BASIC TEXTS IN COUNSELLING AND PSYCHOTHERAPY

Series editor: Stephen Frosh

This series introduces readers to the theory and practice of counselling and psychotherapy across a wide range of topic areas. The books appeal to anyone wishing to use counselling and psychotherapeutic skills and are particularly relevant to workers in health, education, social work and related settings. The books are unusual in being rooted in psychodynamic and systemic ideas, yet being written at an accessible, readable and introductory level. Each text offers theoretical background and guidance for practice, with creative use of clinical examples.

Published

Jenny Altschuler
COUNSELLING AND PSYCHOTHERAPY FOR FAMILIES IN TIMES OF ILLNESS AND DEATH 2nd Edition

Bill Barnes, Sheila Ernst and Keith Hyde
AN INTRODUCTION TO GROUPWORK

Stephen Briggs
WORKING WITH ADOLESCENTS AND YOUNG ADULTS 2nd Edition

Alex Coren
SHORT-TERM PSYCHOTHERAPY 2nd Edition

Jim Crawley and Jan Grant
COUPLE THERAPY

Emilia Dowling and Gill Gorell Barnes
WORKING WITH CHILDREN AND PARENTS THROUGH SEPARATION AND DIVORCE

Loretta Franklin
AN INTRODUCTION TO WORKPLACE COUNSELLING

Gill Gorell Barnes
FAMILY THERAPY IN CHANGING TIMES 2nd Edition

D0221898

Fran Hedges
AN INTRODUCTION TO SYSTEMATIC THERAPY WITH INDIVIDUALS

Fran Hedges
REFLEXIVITY IN THERAPEUTIC PRACTICE

Sally Hodges
COUNSELLING ADULTS WITH LEARNING DISABILITIES

Linda Hopper
COUNSELLING AND PSYCHOTHERAPY WITH CHILDREN AND ADOLESCENTS

Sue Kegerreis
PSYCHODYNAMIC COUNSELLING WITH CHILDREN AND YOUNG PEOPLE

Ravi Rana
COUNSELLING STUDENTS

Tricia Scott
INTEGRATIVE PSYCHOTHERAPY IN HEALTHCARE

Geraldine Shipton
WORKING WITH EATING DISORDERS

Laurence Spurling
AN INTRODUCTION TO PSYCHODYNAMIC COUNSELLING 2nd Edition

Paul Terry
COUNSELLING AND PSYCHOTHERAPY WITH OLDER PEOPLE 2nd Edition

Jan Wiener and Mannie Sher
COUNSELLING AND PSYCHOTHERAPY IN PRIMARY HEALTH CARE

Shula Wilson
DISABILITY, COUNSELLING AND PSYCHOTHERAPY

Steven Walker
CULTURALLY COMPETENT THERAPY

Jenny Walters
WORKING WITH FATHERS

Jessica Yakeley
WORKING WITH VIOLENCE

Invitation to authors

The Series Editor welcomes proposals for new books within the Basic Texts in Counselling and Psychotherapy series. These should be sent to Stephen Frosh at the School of Psychology, Birkbeck College, Malet Street, London, WC1E 7HX (e-mail s.frosh@bbk.ac.uk)

Basic Texts in Counselling and Psychotherapy
Series Standing Order ISBN 0–333–69330–2
(outside North America only)

You can receive future titles in this series as they are published by placing a standing order. Please contact your bookseller or, in the case of difficulty, write to us at the address below with your name and address, the title of the series and the ISBN quoted above.

Customer Services Department, Macmillan Distribution Ltd
Houndmills, Basingstoke, Hampshire RG21 6XS, England

Counselling and Psychotherapy for Families in Times of Illness and Death

2nd Edition

JENNY ALTSCHULER
Consultant Clinical Psychologist and Family Psychotherapist

palgrave
macmillan

First published as Working with Chronic Illness 1997
Reprinted four times
Second edition 2012
PALGRAVE MACMILLAN

Palgrave Macmillan in the UK is an imprint of Macmillan Publishers Limited, registered in England, company number 785998, of Houndmills, Basingstoke, Hampshire RG21 6XS.

Palgrave Macmillan in the US is a division of St Martin's Press LLC, 175 Fifth Avenue, New York, NY 10010.

Palgrave Macmillan is the global academic imprint of the above companies and has companies and representatives throughout the world.

Palgrave® and Macmillan® are registered trademarks in the United States, the United Kingdom, Europe and other countries

ISBN 978–0–230–52100–1

This book is printed on paper suitable for recycling and made from fully managed and sustained forest sources. Logging, pulping and manufacturing processes are expected to conform to the environmental regulations of the country of origin.

A catalogue record for this book is available from the British Library.

A catalog record for this book is available from the Library of Congress.

10   9   8   7   6   5   4   3   2   1
21   20   19   18   17   16   15   14   13   12

Printed and bound in Great Britain by
the MPG Books Group, Bodmin and King's Lynn

CONTENTS

CONTENTS

CONTENTS

ACKNOWLEDGEMENTS

With thanks to the families, colleagues, friends and members of my own family for sharing important aspects of their illness journey with me.

1

INTRODUCTION

Coming to terms with a move from the 'world of the healthy' to the 'world of the ill' (Sontag, 1991) is one of the most difficult challenges we and our families are likely to confront: it shifts us from the domain of the ordinary to the extraordinary, demanding a radical re-organization of our individual, family, social and working lives.

However, our responses to illness are far from uniform. Where the symptoms do not appear to be severe, some (the 'silent and healthy') maintain our usual patterns of behaviour regardless of how we feel, while others (the 'worried well') do the opposite. Similarly, while some ('stoics') tend to underplay symptoms even if they might be indicative of a life-limiting condition others become fully invested in the role of a patient, even if the condition is unlikely to be serious (Lee and Dwyer, 1995).

Families appear to have a powerful influence on our physical and psychological wellbeing, an influence that is equivalent to all standard risk factors associated with illness (Campbell, 2003; Edwards and Clarke, 2004; Knafil and Gillis, 2002). For example, living in the same environment appears to increase the spread of infectious disease; the incidence of respiratory disease is higher in smoking households; and other family patterns such as exercise and diet affect health as well. In addition, research has found that our genetic make-up influences the likelihood of contracting certain conditions, as well as the ability to fight disease (Rolland, 2006; van Riper and Gallo, 2006).

Studies aimed at understanding adjustment to illness highlight the need to take account of social relationships, particularly relationships with one's family. They indicate that negative, critical or hostile relationships have a stronger influence on health than positive relationships, and that experiences of stress (including stresses within the family) affect neuro-endocrine and psycho-immunological pathways, increasing the likelihood of contracting particular conditions (Campbell, 2003; Smith and Glazer, 2006). Moreover, clinical reports suggest that when symptoms (particularly pain) become overwhelming, relationship to these symptoms can assume greater importance than relationships with people one is close to (Mason, 2004). It is therefore surprising that with important exceptions most interventions aimed at treating illness and health care trainings pay relatively little attention to the ways in which families are affected by and affect experiences of illness.

It is also important to note that until recently, a great deal of what was written about illness and death focused on deficit and pathology. This emphasis has helped to establish experiences of illness, disability and death as legitimate areas of study and psychological intervention. However, as with attempts to understand responses to other forms of untimely separation and disruption, war-related trauma, family violence and divorce, it has meant that insufficient attention has been paid to understanding why some people seem able to manage or even thrive in the face of adversity. Nonetheless, there are signs of a shift, as reflected in a growing body of work aimed at identifying factors that mediate risk and reduce the likelihood of a negative chain reaction developing in the face of potentially traumatic circumstances (Brom and Kleber, 2009).

These studies suggest that physical and emotional health is more likely to be compromised when adults and children are exposed to high levels of conflict and criticism; there is a history of psychological trauma; there are additional external stressors; people feel isolated; disease disrupts key developmental experiences; and there is a tendency towards rigidity or perfectionism. In contrast, resilience and healing tends to be greater when the family is cohesive, relationships are mutually supportive, the organization of the family is clear, people are able to communicate openly about the illness, there are few other stressors, caregivers have good coping skills and family beliefs are able to help people retain or regain a sense of hope (Boss, 2006; Rutter, 2006).

In an attempt to address these gaps, this book draws on systemic theory in discussing the challenges individuals and families face when confronted with illness, disability and death, and ways of intervening to help people reflect on their experience and connect with their sense of competence at times of particular difficulty. Although there are important differences between the experience of coming to terms with the disabling consequences of illness, and physical and cognitive disability that results from an accident or military action, many of the issues discussed in relation to illness are equally relevant to these situations.

This first chapter provides the framework for subsequent discussions about clinical work as it outlines the assumptions on which systemic theory is based, how systems respond to change, the challenges associated with ambiguities in roles, tasks and boundaries, and the dynamics that underpin collaboration between medical and non-medical health care professionals. Chapter 2 provides an overall discussion of the main challenges illness, disability and the prospect of death present to individuals and their families, while Chapter 3 draws on a case example in outlining how systemic ideas and techniques can be used to help people move and connect with their sense of competence at times of particular difficulty.

The following six chapters focus on particular aspects of illness, namely the experiences of children, parents, adults and couples, illness in later life, bereavement, and the challenges migration and cross-cultural differences pose to the providers and recipients of health care. The book ends by discussing the personal–professional challenges this work tends to present and how supervision can contribute to the professional development and support of medical and non-medical professionals alike.

To illustrate how systemic ideas and techniques are applied in practice, the book draws on actual clinical experience. However, details have been altered to protect confidentiality and case examples draw on situations that have arisen over the course of the rest of my work to illustrate as wide a range of issues as possible. Although the ideas and techniques discussed here draw on my work as a family psychotherapist and clinical psychologist in a number of inpatient and outpatient health care settings and, more recently, as an independent practitioner, my experience as a supervisor and trainer suggest that they are applicable to the work of other health care professionals, including doctors and nurses.

Introduction to systemic theory

Systemic theory emerged out of a desire to develop ideas and practices that could meet the need to work with families, to move beyond the internal world of the individual to facilitating change in relationships with people who are most significant to them, as well as in their experience of themselves. It draws attention to the centrality of relationships and communication to the development of identity and experience, opening up the possibility of recognizing the interactional ways in which problems are constructed and maintained, rather than seeing problems and 'pathology' as rooted in one person.

The theory has its roots in cybernetics, in the work of scientists who noticed that a wide variety of biological and non-biological phenomena appeared to share the same attributes. This led to attempts to identify a set of principles that could account for the ways in which all systems are organized, maintained, and change in response to internal and external pressures and process information (Bateson, 1972; von Bertalanffy, 1968). Although there are obviously important differences between mechanical, biological and human systems, many of the ideas arising from this original work continue to inform current theorizing and clinical work with families, including that:

- The whole is different from the sum of its parts.
- Change to any one part of a system has a ripple effect on the rest of the system.
- Despite being members of the same system, our experiences of that system are unique.
- Systems (including family and professional systems) respond to disturbances by attempting to re-establish the status quo.
- There is a fine balance between the need for stability and the need to accommodate to change.
- Tensions are more likely to arise at times of transition.
- To understand any observations about a system, one needs to take account of the position of the observer, and the beliefs they hold.

As with all theoretical and therapeutic paradigms, systemic ideas have evolved over time. Subsequent work has moved away from the relatively mechanistic nature of the early theorizing. Although the approach continues to place emphasis on the relational nature of human experience, on interactions in the here and now, increased attention is paid to the individual's internalized experience, including experiences of the past and the ways in which professionals' own experiences affect and are affected by interactions with the people with whom they are working (Byng-Hall, 1985; Flascos and Pocock, 2009).

Informed by social constructionist ideas, current work is based on the assumption that there is an inextricable link between the ways in which we respond, beliefs, language and the discourses that dominate the wider context, including discourses that relate to gender, racialization, age and sexual orientation. Although these wider discourses do not determine how we respond, they inform the range of issues we draw on in knowing and deciding how to act and think. Social constructionsist ideas have also led to growing awareness of the need to take account of the inequalities of power that exist within families and between the recipients and providers of health care (Benbow, 2005; Hollway, 1984; McCann et al., 2000).

Linked with this is the idea of positioning (Davies and Harre, 1999), the idea that in all conversational interactions, we draw on various storylines in presenting a meaningful account of our experience in claiming, affirming, refuting and contesting the ways in which we are positioned by others. Although these positions are not prescriptive, they are informed by the discourses that dominate the context in which these conversational interactions take place. Although positioning is not necessarily intentional and the ways in which we position ourselves and are positioned change depending on the account that is being presented, there are rights and responsibilities associated with a position. This means that being positioned as a patient or carer carries obligations and expectations of how to behave.

Narrative theory has had a significant influence on systemic thinking as well, in particular the idea that experiences are mediated through the stories we tell and are told about ourselves, and that we tend to rework these stories as our experiences and understandings change. This means that, even if certain stories and memories of the past are extremely compelling and powerfully ensconced, one story or memory is never able to embrace the full complexity of the events that take place. As such, other stories, memories and ways of viewing experience are always possible, even if we are unable to see this at the time (Weingarten, 1994; White and Epston, 1990).

With this in mind, a systemic approach to working with people who are ill, disabled and dying is based on the assumption that it is impossible to make sense of experiences of illness, disability and death without taking account of the relationships between the various people concerned (for example, interactions between members of the family, with the health care professionals, friends and colleagues), past experiences of illness and loss, personal and shared beliefs and the discourses that dominate the context in which health care takes place.

However, just because we are part of the same family this does not mean that our responses and views will be the same. Even though a great deal might be shared, our responses, needs, expectations and the level of support we require will differ. This means that when ill people and their families are struggling and become locked into patterns that are troubling to themselves and their loved ones, systemic work involves listening and bearing witness to their distress as well as exploring and uncovering less noticed aspects of their experience. It also means that it is important to take account of the ways in which health care professionals deal with the feelings evoked by ongoing exposure to people who are ill, disabled and likely to die.

How do systems work?

A useful way of understanding how systems work is by thinking in terms of a series of feedback loops, whereby A affects B, B affects C, C affects D and D affects A. These loops operate at all levels of human interaction, from the cellular to the social and political. This opens up the possibility of viewing actions that are understood to be causes as relatively arbitrary punctuations within a complex of interacting cycles. As change at any one level requires a reworking of these patterns of interaction, tensions are more likely to arise at times of transition. In health care settings, this includes times when a child is referred from a paediatric to an adult setting, when someone in the family is unable to fulfil their usual roles and when a member of staff is promoted, leaves or retires.

Anyone who works with illness and disability will be familiar with the idea that the body operates like a system so that injury to any one part of the body can have a 'ripple effect' on the functioning of other parts of the body. For example, an injury to the knee can affect the way in which we stand and walk, impacting on the back and other parts of the skeleton system. If these symptoms become more severe, we may have to rely more on others, affecting our sense of self, our independence and relationships with others. This notion of a ripple effect is integral to understanding the ways in which expected and unexpected change affects the person in question, relationships between family members, and organizational systems, including health care settings.

Viewing actions in this circular way means that, rather than seeing problems, dilemmas or solutions as rooted in one person, they are seen as a reflection of the interactions that take place between two or more people. These interactions include verbal as well as non-verbal interchanges, such as the messages we convey through our tone of voice, and eye contact we do or do not make with others.

This means that in paediatric contexts, instead of seeing the parent of a seriously ill young child's outburst of anger towards the nurse entrusted with the caring for his child as indicative of his character, it needs to be understood as part of a process that involves both parties. We also need to take account of each person's relationships and interactions with others: although this parent's outburst of anger may be an expression of his own feelings, it may also be informed by the anger, frustration and fear of the rest of the family.

The views we hold depend on the position of the observer, and the beliefs that observer holds. With this in mind, the parent's anger may seem unreasonable if understood from the position of a nurse who feels she is doing her best, but from the position of a parent who feels the care their child is receiving is insufficient, that anger is likely to feel quite justifiable.

However, this interaction is likely to be informed by more than one aspect of experience: as such, the parent's anger may reflect his attempt to assert what he sees as in the best interests of his child and the power-lessness of having to rely on others at a time of life when he might otherwise have been able to play a more significant role in caring for his child. Where the condition is terminal, feelings of powerlessness and distress are likely to relate to the feelings evoked by being unable to protect one's child from dying. At such times, the nurse's engagement with this father may be informed by a parallel sense of powerlessness, by the powerlessness of being unable to avert the course of the condition, the more personal fears and anxieties this evokes in her and the difficulty of maintaining a boundary between her personal and profes-sional experience.

As outlined earlier, the beliefs we hold inform the ways in which we think and act. As health care professionals our beliefs about health care will have been informed by our trainings and clinical experience. However, they will also have been informed by more personal experi-ences, including experiences of loss, illness, care and dependency within our own families, and by the ideas about health and illness that dominate the context in which we live. With this in mind, in trying to understand the interchange between this parent and nurse, it is also important to take account of the beliefs of both parties, including beliefs about the roles parents and health care professionals should play when a young child is seriously ill, and the discourses that dominate the context in which this interaction takes place.

For example, if, as I have suggested, the parent in question is a man and the nurse a woman, it might be important to consider how far gendered discourses inform this interchange and the expectations they have of each other. Despite considerable shifts in the positions of men and women, in most but not all cases, mothers tend to assume primary responsibility for the care of a hospitalized child. As such, the father's anger may relate to his difficulty in dealing with a situation in which he feels marginalized. Adding another dimension, if we were to assume that this father is from a minority ethnic group and the nurse is a white British woman, it would also be important to consider how prejudice and racialization impact on their ability to hear one another's views, and the beliefs they have about the likelihood of being heard and respected.

If, however, we were to assume that the professional in question is a doctor, it would also be important to take account of the expectations doctors and others have of their role and positions in society. Most people turn to doctors to guide us, contain our anxiety and save lives when we are ill. Thus doctors tend to command considerable respect. Moreover, because medical consultations tend to take place on territory that is intimidating and unfamiliar to most people (in many cases, where the patient is lying in bed), these experiences can feel disempowering. This sense of disempowerment is reinforced by the fact that, although ill people are only patients in the context of illness, the terms 'patient'[1] and 'doctor' tend to have far reaching implications for the ways in which we see ourselves and are experienced by others.

This is important to bear in mind because although it was previously assumed that a 'good patient' is someone who is compliant, research and clinical experience have alerted us to the risks of dependency, and the value of ensuring that patients hold on to as such of their pre-illness identity and assume as much responsibility for their own care as possible (Barlow et al., 2002; Reiss et al., 1986).

This is not always easy. For example, where an adolescent has a chronic condition, parents and professionals are often faced with balancing two or more contradictory sets of beliefs. At one level, they may recognize that helping the adolescent assume greater responsibility for their own care will allow them to act in a way that is more in keeping with what 'normal' adolescence entails. However, because failure to adhere[2] with the treatment regime can result in a significant deterioration in health, this may feel too dangerous, locking them into a pattern that is uncomfortable for both parties.

Changes in membership and structure of the system

Although all systems tend to respond to these disturbances by attempting to re-establish the status quo, as they operate within the wider context and, in the case of human systems, members of that system change as they become older, the need to re-establish stability has to be balanced with the need to accommodate to change. It is therefore hardly surprising that points of transition tend to be characterized by upheaval and rethinking, as they require changes in patterns of connection (Carter and McGoldrick, 2005).

In most work settings, if an employee leaves, or indeed dies, their post would be advertised with a clear statement about the job specification and personal requirements of any applicant. However, there is rarely any such clarity about the roles and responsibilities of the various family members, or when it might be appropriate for the rest of the family to take over the tasks that had previously lain within the domain of someone who is seriously ill, disabled or even dead.

Some systems continue to operate over a prolonged period of time, as with families, while others are formed to meet specific tasks and dismantled once that task is completed. For example, when a child has a needle phobia, the parent, child, nurse or doctor and possibly a psychologist need to work together to resolve the phobia. Once this has been achieved, that system dissolves and people have to find a way of letting go and re-grouping around other preoccupations.

However, there is often a build up in tension at such times in an attempt to delay or reverse new patterns of relationship, as these changes require a reworking of the ways in which people operate and see themselves. For example, one of the unstated 'rules' of most health care settings is that one needs to carry on working at the same pace even if we have been deeply affected by the experiences of the people with whom we are working, for example by situations in which a young patient has a heart attack or when problems during the birth are likely to have long-term consequences for the child's cognitive ability. In such situations, a common response is for senior staff members to attempt to effect what has been called 'first order change', that is encouraging staff to return to their usual pattern of work. However, the distress evoked in these situations means that trying to underplay how one feels is not only enormously exhausting but impossible, giving rise to such behaviours as absenteeism, listlessness and difficulties in concentrating.

Another possibility is to introduce strategies that allow for the development of a structure that is more compatible with the altered circumstances, 'second order change'. This could involve setting up a session to allow the staff group to debrief, reflect on what took place and make sense of how they feel. This is particularly valuable if the staff group or family have concerns about the quality of family or professional care that a person had received and when there is a possibility that cuts in cost, or racism, ethnicity or sexual orientation, meant that access to care was compromised.

The structure and patterns of relating will need to change as the size and functions of that system develop. For example, many organizations are established and developed as a result of the inspiration and determination of a few people. During what has been called a 'pioneering phase', relationships between the people who work in that project are usually marked by enthusiasm, warmth, loyalty and little formality. As the organization becomes bigger and the demand greater, there is often some form of crisis after which guidelines are established and patterns of communication and accountability need to be clarified to enable the members of that organization to operate. These attempts to establish greater clarity often result in members of the organization feeling they are loosing touch with one another and/or the recipients of the service. Where this is the case, another crisis may arise, leading to restructuring the service once more in a way that allows for a greater level of integration (Campbell et al., 1989).

If, however, the changes that develop are unacceptable, one option we have is to use our voice (Hirschman, 1970) to work towards repairing or improving relationships by communicating complaints, grievances or proposals for change. Another is to withdraw, as in leaving the organization or ending the relationship (as, for example, with divorce), or emotionally, which means investing little energy in the organization without actually leaving the system. Although withdrawing emotionally may be aimed at protecting ourselves and ensuring we have a job, as this is likely to be at odds with the aspirations we have about our work, acting in this way can feel uncomfortable and have problematic implications for the people with whom we work.

Collaborative care and differences in clinical roles

In every job, there are likely to be areas in which we are required to conform to prescribed constraints and others where we need to use our initiative, as at times of unpredictable crises. It can be difficult to achieve the right balance. For example, if we act too independently, we are likely to become, or appear to be, disengaged. Alternatively, if too constrained, we are unlikely to be able to respond creatively. Similarly, although certain aspects of our work are written into our job description, a great deal is not. For example, although the work of each health care professional will be integral to the effective functioning of the unit, we are likely to have different levels of power.

As outlined earlier, despite being members of the same system, our experiences of that system are likely to differ. Amongst members of the family, these differences tend to relate to such factors as age, birth order, gender, personal characteristics like academic ability and particular experiences of the past. Although these factors are applicable to health care professionals as well, other differences relate to our trainings, professional roles, areas of responsibility. These differences may mean that although we share a commitment to working with illness, we have different views about such issues as the value of direct advice, use of technical versus colloquial language, constructions of confidentiality and what the term 'professional boundaries' means.

For example, there are important differences between the skills base, trainings and expectations of medical and mental health professionals. Unlike doctors and nurses, in most health care settings, mental health professionals are not usually required to be 'on call'. However, it is important to respect the reality and constraints of illness and the ways in which health care systems operate. Particularly when working on an inpatient unit, this means being ready to fit sessions around medical procedures like scans and blood tests, and bearing mind that although it may be less burdensome to meet outpatients before or after medical consultations, they are likely to be preoccupied with the information they have just received, or anticipate hearing.

There are also likely to be times when we are required to respond fairly quickly, for example when an emergency psychosocial assessment is needed to assist doctors in deciding whether a discharge is feasible, or when a child who is needle phobic requires an injection. Because the notion of safeguarding the space that has been offered to the people with whom we are working is integral to all forms of counselling and psychotherapy, it may feel inappropriate to cancel or delay sessions that have already been set. However, refusing to do so when it is clear that our services are needed is difficult. It tends to be particularly difficult when trying to establish closer working relationships with our medical colleagues, as this can create the perception that we are uninterested and rarely available. Consequently, it is important to be open about how much time we can offer at the outset of the work and to frame the need for additional psychosocial support as an issue that belongs to the whole team.

Another important difference is that medical and mental health professionals tend to have somewhat different understandings of what confidentiality entails. With the exception of situations where an under age child might be at risk of abuse or severe neglect, maintaining a strict level of confidentiality is integral to all forms of counselling and psychotherapy. This is rooted in the idea that confidentiality is critical to ensuring that people feel able to reflect on issues they find troubling and are unable to address with others. Indeed, in some cases concerns about confidentiality mean people prefer to see someone who has no connection with the treatment team, for fear that the issues they find troubling might compromise their medical care.

In contrast, although medical professionals are also bound by a strict code of confidentiality this does not preclude sharing information with the rest of the treatment team. As such, a counsellor or psychotherapist's decision to withhold information about their sessions can be seen as obstructive. Here too, although it is important to clarify the parameters of how we work at the outset, it is also important to find a compromise that does not jeopardize either aspect of care. This might include encouraging people to share some of the concerns that relate to their health with the rest of the team, or exploring the possibility of doing so on their behalf.

Moreover, with the exception of psychiatrists, and doctors or nurses who opt for a career change, mental health professionals are unlikely to have had a medical training. Despite this, in order to help people make sense of illness-related experience we need to have some understanding of the health-related concerns they are likely to face. This could involve discussing their condition, treatment and likely side effects with medical colleagues, drawing on the literature and reputable Internet sites or asking the affected person and/or family about their condition. However, although this has the advantage of recognizing their expertise and helps to ensure that we will have some understanding of the issues they see as particularly relevant, it does mean that we are unlikely to learn about issues they are unaware of and/or choose to omit. Nonetheless it is important to recognize the limitations of our role and avoid stepping into areas that lie outside of our domain.

The need to respect difference is particularly important at times of referral. The emotional intensity surrounding situations of illness means that the bonds that develop between ill people, their families and the professional tend to be strong. When we have invested time and energy in trying to help people resolve the difficulties they face, a decision to refer them on can feel like a failure and disappointment to the referrer as well as the people who are being referred. Where the referral is from a general practitioner (GP) or consultant to a mental health profession when they have been unable to find an organic cause for the symptoms people experience, it is not unusual for the recipients of their care to feel angry, disappointed and suspicious. Although it may be impossible to fully allay the feelings such referrals arouse, exploring the meanings of the referral to people concerned can go a long way towards helping all parties respect the work that has taken place, reducing the likelihood of confusions developing and sabotaging this next phase of work.

Furthermore, in choosing to work with illness, even if there is considerable respect for psychosocial work, the care of the body is prioritized. This means that as non-medical professionals, there are likely to be times when we are confronted with feelings of powerlessness and are faced with our limitations, when, for example, we are unable to be of any help in relation to the main issue affecting people's lives: a life threatening and debilitating illness. These feelings tend to be heightened at times of crisis, when urgent medical attention is required. Although studies of resilience attest to the importance of being able to reflect on experiences of crisis with someone who can be trusted, people are unlikely to have the mental space to do so until the crisis has abated. There are also likely to be situations where medical professionals fail to recognize or respect what is particular about counselling or psychotherapy, as talking with people is an integral aspect of most caring relationships.

As this discussion suggests, whilst recognizing differences helps to clarify what is particular about our roles and expertise, emphasizing differences tends to obscure what is shared. Conversely, although acknowledging what is shared can be a great help in establishing a comfortable working alliance with colleagues, this can be confusing if it is at the expense of recognizing particular skills and areas of responsibility.

Summary

- A systemic approach to health care is based on the assumption that change to any one part of the system is likely to have a ripple effect on relationships between other members of that system.
- This means that to make sense of experiences of receiving or providing health care, it is important to take account of the context, including interactions with family, friends, colleagues and health care professionals, as well as the beliefs of the various parties involved and the discourses that dominate the society in which health care takes place.
- Factors like differences in health care professionals' roles, tasks and trainings means that the ideas we hold dear are different, creating misunderstandings that can be difficult to understand.
- Rather than negating differences, creative multidisciplinary work relies on a respectful recognition of differences as well as similarities and the value of alternative perspectives.

2

THE IMPACT OF ILLNESS AND DISABILITY ON FAMILIES

Although each person's experiences of illness and disability will be unique, in all cases, we and our families will be faced with coming to terms with the disruptions to our sense of identity and relationships with each other, particularly with the people with whom we are most intimately connected (Bury, 1982; Little et al., 2002).

Most of us are faced with challenges to the ways in which we experience ourselves over the course of our everyday lives. However, what is different about extreme situations like a life-limiting illness is that they tend to threaten our sense of continuity. As such, attempts to restore our sense of who we are and our relationships with others need to take account of the past, present and future we had imagined living (Little et al., 2002; Yngvesson and Mahoney, 2000).

One way of dealing with these discontinuities is by focusing on stable anchor points, by drawing on beliefs and memories that reflect greater continuity between our past, present and future lives. Another is by drawing on and if necessary adapting strategies that were helpful in the past. However, in some cases, the level of incapacitation and life threatening nature of the condition mean that it feels impossible to hold on to aspects of self and patterns of relating that were central to the ways in which we saw ourselves before. For example, where being physically active has been central to our sense of identity, the diagnosis of an incapacitating condition can result in a profound sense of personal alienation as well as a desire to distance ourselves from family and friends for whom this aspect of our lives has been important. Where the ill person is the parent[1] of young children, what tends to be most challenging is the contradictions posed by prioritizing one's own needs over those of one's children.

In other cases, illness becomes a turning point, opening up opportunities to introduce changes that allow for a more fulfilling and comfortable life and relationship with others (Le Shan, 1989). Where relationships have been particularly fraught, the experience of caring or being cared for can lead to a different appreciation of one another and shifting the focus away from past hurts and grievances. Nevertheless, even if being ill opens up the possibility of more positive ways of relating, families have to find a way of:

- Living with the losses and uncertainties illness, disability and threat of death present.
- Balancing acceptance with maintaining some sense of hope.
- Reworking family boundaries.
- Negotiating the demands of the illness with other family needs.
- Holding on to an identity that is not fully consumed by the illness.
- Sharing information with others without invalidating personal privacy.

However, understandings of what 'the family' entails are far from uniform and vary somewhat from culture to culture. Until recently, 'the family' was assumed to refer to a two-parent household in which parents were in a heterosexual relationship, with mothers taking primary responsibility for children. As increased numbers of women work outside the home, divorce rates are higher and more adults are opting for different styles of cohabiting, including living with a partner[2] of the same gender, this image does not fit for a significant proportion of the population. Moreover, in places where mortality is particularly high, for example areas affected by the HIV/AIDs pandemic and war, older children tend to play a far more central role in caring for vulnerable family members than is the case elsewhere.

As importantly, although the term 'family' tends to be used to refer to a biologically linked grouping that spans several generations, and is assumed to be a source of comfort and protection at times of stress and confusion, as reflected in reports of family violence and neglect this is not always the case.

Shared and individual experiences of loss

Attachment theory, with its roots in studies of infant and young children's responses to being separated from a primary caretaker, has had a significant impact on understandings of responses to loss (Bowlby,

1953, 1980). This body of work indicates that where there is a history of secure attachment and family members are well supported, people are more able to adjust to the losses that occur in later life, and where attachment has been less secure, they are more vulnerable to the potentially destructive effect subsequent losses can present. This suggests that responses to the losses associated with being ill and loss of a loved one are likely to be informed by ways in which these earlier experiences were negotiated. However, this is not always the case: where other members of the family have been diagnosed with and died as a result of a life-limiting condition, there is likely to be heightened fear associated with the diagnosis of the same condition, even if there is a history of secure attachment (Rolland, 1994).

The work of Kubler-Ross (Kubler-Ross, 1970) has also had a considerable effect on current understandings of loss. Her work suggests that faced with any significant loss, we tend to go through a series of stages including *denial* (a conscious or unconscious refusal to accept the facts, information, and reality of the situation concerned), *anger* (anger at ourselves and/or others, especially people with whom we are closest), *bargaining* (for example, attempting to bargain with whatever spiritual source we believe in or had believed in before), *depression* (a form of preparatory grieving, a sadness and regret, fear, and sense of uncertainty that heralds an acceptance of reality) and *acceptance* (a move towards greater emotional detachment and objectivity).

The staged-based nature of her model suggests that patterns that are adaptive at certain stages may be less so at others. For example, although denial offers a way of managing the chaos and confusion that tends to set in following the diagnosis of a life-limiting condition, if this continues, a process of mutual pretence is likely to develop, isolating people from each other at a time when they are likely to benefit most of all from being able to turn to one another for support.

However, our responses to loss tend to be more varied than this model suggests. For example, when someone is diagnosed with a serious illness or dies, some of us try to deny what is happening and hold on to our pre-illness identity and lives, some focus more of their energy on preparing for the worst and others oscillate between periods of intense grief and periods when it is more possible to get on with the rest of our lives (Lee and Dwyer, 1995). Similarly, while some seek solace from spirituality, others focus more of their energies on diet, exercise and other self-help activities (Koenig et al., 2001).

Moreover, although some of the challenges ill and healthy members of the family face are similar, there are also important differences, including differences in power and dependency. Although underplaying differences can help families maintain some sense of continuity in a context that tends to be dominated by uncertainty and disruption, this is problematic if it means one or all members of the family need to subsume their own needs. It also tends to create a sense of artificiality that limits the possibility of maintaining that sense of relational continuity. Unacknowledged, these differences can find expression in guilt about being able bodied, feelings of resentment about the burden of care and, for those who are ill, about the greater freedom of movement other family members have. Conversely, although acknowledging difference allows for greater openness, if this means denying what is shared, there is a greater chance of suffering and caring responsibilities becoming the primary way of seeing things with one another.

Recognizing what is shared and different tends to be more complicated when the illness offers healthy family members opportunities that were less available before, as often occurs when one member of a couple is seriously ill. Feminist studies has led to the understanding that instead of feminine and masculine identities being absolutes, they are more accurately regarded as 'floating signifiers' (Lévi-Strauss, 1987), with men and women occupying two ends along a particular social continuum (Hollway, 1984; Winther Jørgensen and Phillips, 2002). Nonetheless, although shifts in patterns of employment and care have led to a greater sense of parity within many work settings, within the home, mothers tend to be expected to assume primary responsibility for the care of young children and other vulnerable dependants.

This means that in the case of heterosexual couples, where a mother is seriously ill, her partner is likely to assume more responsibility for caring for their children than before. Whilst this shift might present practical difficulties, it can allow fathers to develop a closer relationship with their children, altering their experience of themselves. In contrast, when the father is ill, the mother is likely to have to assume responsibility for tasks that had fallen within his domain before. As most societies place a higher value on the tasks associated with male roles, the shift is likely to result in mothers being able to see themselves and respect their own voice in a different way (Dale, 1997).

When the person who had been ill recovers, the healthy partner is likely to feel forced to relinquish their new role to help their partner regain aspects of identity that had been central to who he or she had been before. However, if adopting this role has led to a more positive understanding of oneself, relinquishing this role may be a real loss. Parents who are in a same-sex relationship face similar challenges. Although they are often less bound by traditional gendered roles, because many prize a greater sense of parity, the shifts in power and dependency tend to be particularly difficult. As such, it can be helpful to explore what both parties have learned over this period in order to help them move on.

Boss's (2006) studies of families in which one person has Alzheimer's disease or works for the military and is 'missing' draw attention to the difficulties of coming to terms with ambiguous forms of loss, as when someone is 'emotionally present' but 'psychologically absent' or the reverse, 'physically absent' but 'emotionally present'. Being able to view someone who is cognitively impaired as a real presence can help the family maintain a sense of continuity and allows that person to be seen as someone whose identity is not only defined in terms of disease and deficit. However, difficulties are likely to arise if this means denying reality and failing to organize family roles to accommodate to their altered level of functioning.

Being able to view those who are physically absent as an ongoing presence can be enormously sustaining as well. This is reflected in the comfort children experience from being able to speak to hospitalized parents on the phone, having them sing or read to them at bedtime. It is likely to account for the comfort they experience from having a 'transitional object' (Winnicott, 1971) like a teddy bear that signifies parents' presence and containment. In addition, viewing those who are absent as a psychological presence allows families to draw on the views they imagine that person would have had in reaching decisions about care. However, because they are not actually present, it is impossible to know how they might react to these circumstances. It also tends to limit their readiness to establish and draw on a new supportive network (Rolland, 1994).

Blame and responsibility

Faced with situations we cannot understand, one of the most common responses is to ask ourselves 'why?' The work of Klein (1975) and later Benjamin (1998) suggests that faced with situations of loss and uncertainty, one way of protecting ourselves is to project what is feared or hated onto someone else or a different situation entirely.

In contexts of illness, this may take the form of distancing ourselves from our own bodies and/or viewing the body as an unreliable but indispensable vehicle rather than an integral part of who we are. This tendency is reflected in the use of such terms as 'it' or 'the' disease rather than the more personal 'me', 'I' or 'my'. It can also take the form of projecting blame onto other members of the family or the inadequacy of the health care service or, in the case of healthy members of the family, distancing oneself from the person who embodies what is hated or feared.

Another way of responding to loss and uncertainty is by blaming oneself. The inclination to blame oneself tends to be informed by particular personal and family experiences as well as the beliefs that dominate the societies in which we live. For example, in western society, there is a tendency to believe that we have the ability to determine our own health status by following the correct diet, or exercise regime, and adopting certain attitudes of mind. This is reflected in the idea that adopting a 'fighting spirit' towards cancer increases the chances of healing and survival (Greer, 2000; Seligman, 1996).

Although I would not want to suggest that mental attitudes have no impact on health and wellbeing, framing the ability to 'fight' cancer as lying within one's control means that when the disease reoccurs, the person in question has to come to terms with the fact that they are not only extremely ill but that they are to blame. Moreover, much of the evidence supporting this idea relies on anecdotes or re-describing results showing a correlation as indicators of cause, and ignores the fact that the cause and process of disease are multi-factorial.

Questions of blame and personal control are particularly important to bear in mind when working with conditions where there is an established link with smoking (as with certain respiratory conditions including emphysema), alcohol abuse (cirrhosis) and other life style choices. Indeed, research suggests that some people who know they have a heart disease delay seeking medical care when unwell because they believe they will be criticized for failing to take care of their health (Richards et al., 2003).

Concerns about being criticized or blamed are also important to bear in mind when stress is seen as a major contributor (as with Crohn's disease, chronic fatigue syndrome and certain heart conditions) and when people are suffering from symptoms for which no organic cause can be found. The latter situation is particularly difficult (even if some organic cause is found at a later date in some cases). However, where expressions of emotional distress and the issues people find troubling are seen to bring shame on the family (including experiences of abuse), somatizing may be the only way of expressing this distress.

The tendency to blame oneself for being ill (or the person who is ill) is more prevalent when the ill person is an adult. In contrast, when children are ill, parents and other adults are more likely to be held accountable. Although parents carry considerable responsibility for their children's wellbeing, holding one parent (more often the mother) fully responsible ignores the role other caretakers, environmental factors and interactions with other significant adults and peers play. Ascriptions of blame also appear to be gendered. For example, men are more likely to blame external factors and women to blame themselves. This is reflected in the 'mother blaming' that dominates much of the psychological literature and seems to underpin the tendency to direct a greater proportion of health care initiatives towards women (Weingarten, 1994).

Ambiguities in family boundaries

Regardless of whether we live in a two or three generational household with one or two parents or other relatives, most families construct a relatively impermeable boundary between themselves and the outside world. The strength of that boundary varies from family to family and culture to culture: for example, family boundaries tend to be far stronger in western societies than in societies that prioritize a greater sense of interdependence and connection with the community.

However, when someone is seriously ill the boundary becomes more permeable to allow doctors, nurses and other health care professionals to provide the medical care that is needed. Where a child is hospitalized and there are two parents, one parent (usually but not always a mother) tends to assume primary responsibility for the ill child, and the other for the rest of their children. Even though this might present practical challenges, for an initial period, concerns about survival mean that this presents relatively little difficulty. Tensions are more likely to arise when this pattern continues for longer because the system that is most important, the system which focuses on survival, excludes the rest of the family, including the other parent. As this is not deliberate but a consequence of trying to ensure that the ill child receives the best care possible and the needs of the rest of the family are respected, it can be difficult to acknowledge the discomfort of feeling excluded (Walker, 1983).

Because transitions tend to be accompanied by upheaval and a reworking of how we see ourselves and relate to others, it is not unusual for tensions to escalate at such times (Carter and McGoldrick, 2005). For example, couples often find it possible to be there for one another during crisis phases but more difficult when the crisis abates and they face the need to return to some semblance of 'normality'. Tensions can also arise when the boundaries between the family and others change to accommodate to the demands the illness places on family life. The need for additional practical as well as emotional support means that the boundary between the rest of the family, friends and school may need to become more permeable as well. For example, because teachers can play a pivotal role in helping children who have been absent re-engage with school, catch up on academic work and renegotiate their relationship with peers. Families need to be more open with school about aspects of their lives they had seen as private before. However, this may run counter to the image people have of themselves and the way in which they view dependency on others.

Challenges that relate to the condition in question

To understand the challenges individuals and their family are facing, it is important to take account of the actual condition in question, including the nature of the condition's onset, course, likely prognosis and level of incapacitation (Rolland, 1994).

For example, in some situations, the onset of a condition is extremely gradual, as is usually (but not always) the case with multiple sclerosis and Parkinson's disease. In others the onset is far more acute, as with a heart attack or deep vein thrombosis. Although certain aspects of readjustment, problem solving and emotional demands will be similar, acute conditions tend to require a more rapid mobilization of family resources and intense involvement with professionals.

Where the onset is gradual, families are able to mobilize in a less hurried way. However, because it tends to be more difficult to notice a gradual deterioration, at a later point the individual and family might be faced with feelings of regret, guilt and frustration about their inability to recognize this before, particularly where confusion about changes in behaviour meant that relationships had become increasingly fraught. In some cases the feelings evoked by the ways in which the family responds during this initial phase may be short lived. However, in others they have a longer lasting effect on the extent to which illness and disability come to organize family members' relationships with one another (Rolland, 1994).

When someone has a stroke, families tend to be faced with an initial crisis that requires an enormous adjustment in roles. Once the crisis has abated, the condition tends to stabilize, allowing the family to readjust their roles. Where the condition follows a progressive course, families tend to experience little relief in demand and are required to adapt and change repeatedly. In contrast, where the illness is episodic or relapsing, periods of good health enable some family activities and rituals to be maintained or restored.

However, the transitions between crisis and non-crisis require a repeated reworking of roles and expectations of oneself and others. As such, where families appear to be struggling, normalizing the sense of panic and confusion that tends to arise at such times can go a long way towards framing responses that are seen to reflect deep seated differences as an almost inevitable response to crisis and as the consequence of having to renegotiate one's roles and expectations.

Needless to say, the level of incapacitation and symptom visibility has a profound impact on people's sense of identity and intimate relationships (Kleinman, 1998; Mattingley, 1998). For example, with conditions like motor neuron disease, in advanced stages the affected person is likely to remain cognitively intact but have problems in communicating. This means that they have difficulties in expressing what they want and need. It also means that it is difficult for the rest of the family to know whether to separate, grieve, or help the diagnosed person retain their position within the family.

It is also important to take account of the ways in which the condition in question is viewed by the rest of society. For example, as reflected in the lack of any agreed form of terminology, ambiguity about the extent to which psychological and physiological factors contribute to the cause and course of chronic fatigue, myalgic encephalomyelitis (ME) or post-viral syndrome, means that it is often more difficult for people who have this condition to be recognized as ill and know how to pace themselves.

Nevertheless our responses to these situations are far from uniform. For example, we tend to prioritize somewhat different aspects of experience: one woman said she was able to come to terms with the debilitating impact multiple sclerosis was having and would have on her in the future. However, what she found far more difficult to deal with was that her adolescent daughter was embarrassed by her clumsy gait and so was unwilling to be seen out with her. Similarly, where the condition is potentially life threatening, some of us tend to respond by seeking as much intimacy as possible, while others try to protect one another from the pain of parting, by distancing themselves from loved ones. Indeed, fears of death may take over as much when chances of survival are higher (for example with asthma) as when survival rates are poor.

Although a number of factors are likely to account for these differences, as discussed earlier, current experiences of loss and uncertainty can trigger feelings that relate to far earlier experiences. This means that regardless of whether we or someone close to us is seriously ill, we may be dealing with feelings that relate to two experiences: one that relates to the present situation and the other to the past. Where these feelings relate to experiences of neglect, abuse and powerlessness, the forced sense of intimacy that arises from being cared for by close family can feel enormously intrusive. This is particularly difficult when the memory of these experiences has been blocked out of consciousness and emerges as flashbacks that are terrifying and hard to understand. It is also more difficult where the desire to avoid the present being contaminated by the past means that we have not shared these experiences with the people we are most connected with in the present (Herman, 1997).

Although recalling these memories can be distressing, talking about them with someone who is trusted can help people reach a more comfortable understanding of past and present relationships and the challenges they face in coming to terms with the consequences of being ill, for example dependence on others. Some might find talking about the past too painful and fear this could compound the struggles they are already facing. Nonetheless, where people's sense of panic or fear of dependency seems to be out of proportion, it is worth bearing in bear in mind that their responses may be informed by past experience, even if this is not addressed openly.

Challenges associated with the treatment

The nature of the actual treatment informs individual and families' experiences of illness. In some cases, the consequences of treatment are short lived, as with the side effects of a limited course of medication. In others they are far more long lasting, as when one requires a mastectomy or when removal of a brain tumour results in cognitive deficit.

In many cases, the diagnosis of a chronic condition means that the affected person is required to adhere with a particular treatment regime. This may include having to take medication at prescribed times, altering one's diet, or other life style changes such as increasing or reducing one's levels of activity.

Problems with adherence tend to place an enormous strain on relationships and often result in the rest of the family becoming increasingly watchful of that person's intake of medication, food, and level of activity, affecting their sense of personal control and relationships within the family. They tend to place an additional burden on health care professionals: because the person concerned is likely to be more unwell than is necessary, they require additional professional support, impacting on other people's access to care.

Concerns about the potentially disempowering effect of having to abide by a strict regime of treatment have led to placing greater emphasis on self-management, on encouraging the affected adult or adolescent to adopt more responsibility for their own health care (Barlow et al., 2002; Newman et al., 2009). This requires a careful assessment of the person's emotional and cognitive capacity, physiological status, understanding of the treatment and life style changes required. In some cases they and their families need additional support to help them resolve the ambivalence associated with the changes that are needed.

Although it might seem logical to assume people will do everything to maximize the chances of healing and survival, most of us experience some ambivalence about being forced to change personal habits and ways of behaving that are intrinsic to our sense of identity, particularly changes that might limit our autonomy. However, because adolescence is a time when in most societies people become increasingly independent and questioning of authority, ambivalence about change tends to be more pronounced. As such, where adolescents are concerned, the work also needs to include an assessment of parents' readiness to support such a shift and exploration of what needs to change before they feel confident to help their daughter or son assume greater responsibility.

Worries about the costs of non-adherence mean that it is common for parents and professionals to stress the negative consequences of the person's behaviour and respond with such terms as 'you must' and 'you should' when someone seems unable or unwilling to maximize their chances of healing and survival. However, rather than increasing adherence, adopting this stance tends to be experienced as disempowering and can result in increasing their resistance to change.

With this in mind it is important to adopt a collaborative approach in outlining the rationale for the treatment, what is required from the person concerned and the likely consequences of non-adherence, in a more collaborative way. Where there are problems with adherence, instead of being critical it is more helpful to ask the person concerned open-ended questions aimed at understanding the person's own concerns, increasing their awareness of the problems associated with their current life style, the consequences they are experiencing or are likely to experience, and creating greater optimism about the possibility to change (Miller and Rollnick, 2002).

It is also important to be realistic, offer as much choice as possible (such as choice in relation to times of medication and sorts of activities that are likely to be more manageable) and take account of the person's interactions with others. For example in the case of adolescents, this might mean encouraging parents to create opportunities for them to express their autonomy that are less risky to health.

One of the other challenges families face is that in certain circumstances the treatment challenges taken-for-granted ideas about child care and personal boundaries. This is true of situations in which parents are required to apply aggressive physiotherapy to children with cystic fibrosis and/or change a catheter that is close to their groin. In some situations it is also difficult to separate the physiological from the psychological. For example, where a member of the family has Parkinson's disease, behaviours that appear to be indicators of boredom or a lack of concentration may be indications that the effectiveness of their medication has worn off and they are due for the next dose.

Continuing advances in technology are raising new challenges for families and professionals alike. For example, in the past, children with end stage renal failure were required to take time off from school in order to receive haemodialysis in hospital, affecting their opportunities to learn, relationships with peers, and parents' ability to be there for the rest of their family. Increased access to dialysis at home has eased this. However, it has also meant that parents are having to assuming responsibility for procedures that carry a high risk of infection. The fact that transplants are more feasible is also confronting families with dilemmas that were unknown before, such as how to weigh up the possibility of donating one's organ with the risk this might cause to their own health. In addition, although there is a higher possibility that a family member's kidney, bone marrow or liver sample will be a good enough match, the success or failure of the transplant is likely to have an effect on relationships between the ill person, the donor and the rest of the family (Crombie and Franklin, 2006).

Finally, the notion of prior trauma discussed above is equally relevant to understanding responses to treatment. For example, in many treatment situations, such as chemotherapy, the person concerned is required to assume a fairly passive role. If one has been sexually abused, lying passively while tubes are inserted into one's body can reawaken feelings that relate to this earlier experience of invasion. Similarly, where people have experienced extreme forms of incarceration, as with Nazi concentration camps, the experience of watching one's body become increasingly emaciated can trigger flashbacks of events people had blocked out or tried to deny in order to get on with their lives.

The course of the condition

As discussed in relation to loss, it used to be assumed that most medical conditions follow a relatively set series of phases: initial, chronic and terminal, and that patient, family and professional roles shift in a similar way as the condition deteriorates. However, the notion of set phases fails to take account of the unpredictability of human responses and factors like co-morbidity and variability in symptom progression.

Nonetheless, certain patterns tend to be more common. At the outset, there is often a period when a person experiences unusual or ambiguous sensations but does not know how seriously to take them. If these sensations fail to abate or become more severe, their attention (and the attention of people close to them) tends to focus more on the body, these sensations start to be seen as indicators of disease, and decisions are take about whom to tell.

Diagnosis is usually the first time that the professional, the affected person and (particularly with young children and vulnerable adults), another member of their family meet. These initial meetings tend to set the terms and tone of future collaboration. The shock of finding out one is seriously ill can make it extremely difficult to process and remember what is said. As such, it can be helpful to attend such consultations with a person one can trust as it means that someone else is able to hear what is said and ask the questions one does not think about at the time. Nonetheless, many people prefer to process this information on their own before sharing this with others. It is worth mentioning that although considerable attention has been paid to training health professionals on how to share 'bad' news with adults and children, parents who are told they have a life-limiting condition, for example breast cancer, are rarely offered a chance to reflect on how to share this with their children and the impact their condition might have on their relationship (Barnes et al., 2000).

During this initial phase, the boundary of the family needs to become more permeable in order to maximize the chances of survival, and points of crisis tend to be accompanied by a sense of panic. The energies of the family and health professionals focus on essential forms of assessment and life support at these times, with professionals acting in an authoritative way, drawing on their technical skills and providing comfort and information. While the person concerned has to form an alliance with the medical team, follow orders and learn how to deal with their symptoms and the consequences of the treatment required, the rest of the family needs to be flexible enough to support that person and the treatment they require.

Depending on the course of the condition, the family are then faced with rebuilding their lives in a way that takes account of present disruptions in family roles and routines, as well as altered expectations of the future. This tends to require reworking relationships with the rest of the family and friends to regain a greater sense of privacy and control over their own lives. Following this, many conditions enter a more chronic phase. Over this time, relationships with medical professionals tend to be less intense, allowing the boundary between family and professionals to return an approximation of where it had been before. In some cases, the family needs to play a part in monitoring the person's health, assisting with procedures that take place in the home, coming to terms with relational shifts and the restrictions the illness poses to their individual and shared lives (Rolland, 1994).

Although it is not unusual for tensions to escalate, released from the crisis, the reality begins to set in. Depending on the nature of the condition, families may be faced with such challenges as balancing care giving with personal needs for intimacy and autonomy, other family needs, and coming to terms with feelings of loss and despair.

Advances in care mean that, as with many forms of cancer, the treatment results in cure, and the 'survivor' and their family face the tasks of restoring and preserving aspects of self and family that had been integral to their sense of self and family before. However, as with the initial diagnosis, responses tend to vary: whilst some survivors are able to do so with relatively little difficulty or find that the experience allows them to rework their lives in a way that feels more satisfactory to themselves and their family, for others life remains dominated by loss, alienation and a sense of foreboding (Little et al., 2002; Zebrack, 2000).

Where the person's condition deteriorates and it becomes clear that they will not survive, as the treatment shifts to palliative care, there is often a change in who is included in reaching decisions. As feelings of grief, separation and mourning increase, some family members begin to accept that the end is near and others panic or move into action as if trying to deny reality. While some find solace in religious and spiritual beliefs, others do not. Where the dying person had been the one to hold the family together, as is often the case with parents, their impending death forces the rest of the family to rethink their relationship with one another. Despite the image that families pull together at such times, where relationships have been particularly problematic these problems may assume increased importance. Although the emotional intensity that surrounds situations of death can create a different understanding of the past, this is not always feasible: instead feelings of anger, guilt, regret and blame can become so dominant that they overshadow the possibilities of reaching a more comfortable resolution before parting.

Age and the life cycle of the family

Most of the earlier attempts to understand how relationships change as family members become older were aimed at establishing patterns that could apply to all families. However, increased awareness of the diverse ways in which families are organized and respond to change means that this idea is now recognized as over simplistic. Nonetheless, certain tendencies are useful to bear in mind.

Despite cultural and individual variations, most families move through periods in which there is greater or less closeness and cohesion as their members become older. During early child rearing, the attention of the family (including grandparents) tends to focus inwards, reflecting a pull Combrinck-Graham (1985) calls 'centripetal'. As children reach adolescence, the attention tends to shift towards greater engagement with relationships that are external to the family, reflecting a more 'centrifugal' pull. This usually shifts to focus inwards once more as parents and other older members of the family reach later life.

When someone is seriously ill, as described in relation to early child rearing, the attention of the family tends to focus inwards. Where this inward shift coincides with anticipated age-related patterns, there is likely to be less disruption to anticipated family roles. However, there is also a greater risk of the preoccupations of the family remaining focused inwards despite subsequent changes in health status. In contrast, when the pull of the illness is at odds with anticipated roles, families have to find a way of negotiating the contradictions between age-expected aspirations and patterns of relating with the constraints of the illness and its treatment.

For example, adolescence is a time when, particularly in the west, young people tend to focus more of their energies on relationships with peers and situations that are unrelated to the parents. However, the diagnosis of a serious illness at this time in life means that opportunities for independence are less feasible as they are likely to need to be more reliant on parents than they or their parents had imagined. Indeed, although there may be times when they may want and need to turn to parents for practical and emotional support, the dissonance between what is seen to be 'normal' and lived experience means that doing so feels uncomfortable or even shameful. Adding to the complexity is that although adolescents tend to become increasingly preoccupied with their bodies and have a greater desire for more privacy at such times, their condition may affect their appearance and their parents may need to be involved in intimate aspects of their care.

As young people form new relationships, one of the main tasks they face (particularly in western societies) is establishing a greater sense of independence from their family of origin. When illness strikes at this stage of life, the emotional intensity associated with the illness can bring couples closer to one another than before. However, particularly when the relationship is relatively new and there are financial worries, it is not unusual for the ill partner to become increasingly engaged with their family of origin. This means that in addition to coming to terms with the impact illness may have on their present and future lives, young people find themselves drawn into a closer relationship with their family of origin, which can be difficult for them and their partner to accept and manage. This is particularly problematic when parents had disapproved of their relationship in the first place.

As discussed in Chapter 8, when illness strikes in later life, families face a somewhat different set of challenges. For example, regardless of when one becomes ill, the almost moral value western societies ascribe to being healthy and the shame that is associated with breaching certain social norms mean that it is hardly surprising that people feel ashamed of the loss of control, helplessness and incapacitation associated with many medical conditions. However, the neurological impairments that cause memory loss and behaviours that would otherwise be seen as breaching social norms are far more common in later life, as is the case with symptoms of Alzheimer's disease and vascular dementia (Curtis and Dixon, 2005; Surbone et al., 2006).

Moreover, even if partners have been able to look to one another for support in the past, being older means there is more chance that partners will have died or are too frail to be able to offer the sort of support that is needed. When one's partner's health deteriorates to the point that residential care is needed, the healthier partner will be faced with deciding whether or not to follow them into residential care. Adult children, more often daughters, tend to become more involved at such times. Where they are still responsible for caring for their own children, balancing these dual sets of responsibilities can be extremely stressful. As such, they may find it helpful to reflect on how to negotiate these competing sets of responsibilities with someone outside of the family. However, it is also important to recognize that caring for a parent or being cared for by an adult child can be deeply satisfying to both parties: where parent–child relationships have been extremely fraught, it can lead to a different understanding of each other as well as of themselves.

The impact of illness on communication

In medical contexts, the chances of healing and survival tend to rely on concrete facts, for example on exact measures of blood pressure, body temperature, levels of sugar in the blood, and taking set amounts of medication at prescribed intervals. As such, the sharing and under-standing of these sorts of information is an important feature of health care and making sense of what the illness means to oneself and others.

Over time, most families reach an unstated agreement on how much to disclose to one another. However, when someone in the family is seriously ill, this agreement often needs to change to allow members of the family to develop a shared understanding of what they want and need from each other, confront the possibility of death, decide what to say to others, and agree on the life style changes that are needed to maximize the chances of healing and minimize suffering.

Most of us fluctuate in how much we wish to know, acknowledge, and what we feel we can, want or should share with others. For exam-ple, many brush off conversations about dying or settling affairs with humour. Humour can be helpful in the short term as it allows us to hold on to aspects of life that are not only about illness, disability and death. However, if this becomes the only way of operating, it can limit the possibility of holding on to a real sense of connection, blocking off the chances of addressing more serious issues and paralysing decision-making.

There are obviously many situations where there is an understand-able desire to place a 'protective filter' (Judd, 1989) on what is shared, particularly with members of the family we see as particularly fragile. As professionals as well as family members, it can feel difficult and even inappropriate to raise issues we know others would find troubling when they are in great pain, dependent on us for care, or when it is someone on whom we depend for care. It is also understandable that one may want to assimilate what has been said before sharing this with others.

However, particularly where the thoughts and feeling we have are deeply troubling, they tend to be transmitted in an unlanguaged way, through gesture, eye contact and the ways in which we speak. This means that the people with whom we interact are likely to be faced with contradictory messages. Indeed, in the absence of being told what is happening, we tend to construct our own stories, leading to understandings that may be far more frightening than the reality we face.

In a context that tends to be dominated by concrete information and medical facts, it is easy to underplay the healing power of sharing one's concerns without having to defend how we feel or what we think. Indeed, the need to talk about experiences we find troubling seems to relate to a deep need to make sense of what is happening to us, and to be understood by ourselves as well as by others (Bruner, 1990; Frankl, 1984). However, it is also important to recognize that although speaking openly about illness and death is currently viewed as best practice in most western societies, this idea is relatively new. It is also antithetical to people who have moved from societies that do not share these beliefs, where the idea of withholding how one feels, avoiding telling someone they are dying, and speaking in a more indirect or obscure way is not dishonest but indicative of a different appreciation of respectful and ethical care (Candib, 2002). As such, we need to tread carefully and avoid pushing people into sharing information on how they think and feel until they are ready to do so.

Summary

- Although each person's and each family's experience of illness will be unique, the diagnosis of a life-limiting medical condition demands a radical re-organization in how we see ourselves and relate to others.
- The diagnosis of a life-limiting condition tends to face people with:
  o The need to find a way of living with uncertainty and loss
  o Balancing acceptance with maintaining hope
  o Negotiating the demands of the illness and its treatment with the needs of the family
  o Reworking family boundaries
  o Holding on to other aspects of identity
  o Deciding what can and cannot be shared with others.
- Although resilience tends to be enhanced where there is open communication, we need to tread carefully and avoid pushing people into sharing information and how they think and feel until they are ready.

3

APPLYING SYSTEMIC IDEAS TO HEALTH CARE

This chapter draws on the example of work with one family to illustrate how systemic ideas can be applied to working with families facing illness. Many people do not want or need additional support at times of illness and find strength they were unaware of or feel supported by family and friends in ways that seemed unimaginable before. Nevertheless, there are times when almost everyone would find it helpful to reflect on the challenges they face, with someone who is not part of their family, particularly someone involved in caring for them or a loved one. However, medical professionals are rarely able to offer such support on anything other than an occasional basis and do not always feel equipped in dealing with the more complicated psychosocial consequences being ill poses to people.

As such, where people appear to be struggling or request additional support, it may be preferable for them to see a counsellor or psychologist who has experience of work with illness. Additional psychosocial support tends to be needed where there are signs of high levels of anxiety, hostility and deep despair; an inability to resolve conflicts and reach decisions about care; chaotic or overly rigid family patterns that inhibit people's ability to deal with stress and respond flexibly to the challenges they face; an inability to hear one another; a level of closeness that precludes the possibility of the ill person (or another family member) experiencing some sense of autonomy; relationships that are so distant that physical and emotional needs are not met; unresolved issues that pre-date the illness; and patterns of interacting that are abusive.

For example, Rachael aged 46 was referred to an outpatient child and family mental health clinic by her GP following a consultation in which she shared her worries about the effect her diagnosis of a disseminating form of cancer was having on her children, Sandra (15), Pete (12) and Lucy (5), herself and her partner Andrew.

During an initial phone call, I learnt that Rachael was particularly worried about Sandra and Lucy. Although Sandra had been extremely helpful during the earlier stages of her disease, she had started to act in a rude and aggressive way towards her mother. Rachael was finding it increasingly difficult to discipline her younger child, Lucy. However, she ended by saying that her husband was finding the strain of supporting her and their children too much. She also felt he was finding it difficult to cope with how much she had changed and was afraid he might leave her. We ended with the decision to invite the whole family to an initial consultation. Thereafter, the work included sessions with the whole family, sessions with the couple, individual sessions with the parents, and on one occasion, a session with the older two children.

As with all systemic work, primary emphasis was placed on the immediate problems they were facing, and on the patterns of relationships that seemed to be maintaining these problems. However, as past experiences can have a profound effect on responses to the present, there were times when the work included exploring the links between the present and past.

Setting the context and agreeing on the contract of work

In trying to help people make sense of their emotional concerns, it is preferable to meet in a private space where there are unlikely to be any interruptions. In some cases, inpatients are unable to get out of bed. If so it is important to create as much privacy as possible, for example by drawing the curtains. Where they are more mobile, it is best to meet in a room that is on or close to their ward, particularly if they are on a drip or immobile for other reasons. However, lack of space often means that these discussions need to take place elsewhere and in most cases in a child or adult psychiatry department. Where this is the case, it is important to discuss the significance of the location to dispel concerns that they are considered to be mentally unwell.

Regardless of where people are seen, it is important to explore and clarify the aims and confines of our work together. In this case, this meant sharing the fact that unlike their GP, I was not available 'on call'. However, it was also important to respect the reality and constraints of the illness as there were times when sessions needed to be cancelled at the last minute when Rachael felt too ill to attend, and some of this work took place on the telephone.

One of the other issues we needed to address at the outset was confidentiality. This included clarifying that unless concerns about child protection emerged, the confidentiality of what was shared in these sessions would be preserved. However, as several other professionals, particularly the GP, were involved in Rachael's care, it was also important to discuss what could and could not be shared with the rest of the team.

As the GP he had known the family for some time and would continue to be involved in their care, although he had sent a referral letter, it was enormously helpful to discuss his concerns by phone. Personal introductions go a long way towards ensuring that the referrer feels heard, and limits the likelihood of the referred person feeling they have been 'passed on' or have failed. Although telephone calls are not always feasible, they can also alert us to areas of differences, enabling us to establish where the boundaries of our various roles should lie. However, in some cases, instead of working directly with the family, they suggest that it might be preferable to offer the referrer a consultation about their own engagement with that person.

Developing hypotheses

Most of us develop hypotheses about one another over the course of our everyday lives, hypotheses that guide us on how to respond and what to expect. Acknowledging the hypotheses we hold and testing them out can offer important insights about people's concerns and preoccupations (Boscolo et al., 1987). For example, when someone is referred, or chooses to introduce personal concerns, during the course of a medical consultation, useful questions to consider include:

- *Why now*, why have they been referred for additional psycho-social support now (or in the case of discussions that take place during medical consultations, why are they asking for help with this particular issue now)?
- *What* is the referrer, this person and the rest of their family most concerned about?
- *Why* did the family, parent or professional decide to approach this particular service for help?

Knowing who motivated the referral offers us some clue as to who is the most concerned about the current situation, and who might have most to gain or lose from the changes that have taken, or will take place. The fact that Rachael had approached her GP suggested that she was most keen on change. Had the referral been at the behest of someone else, for example a teacher who was worried about one of the children, I would have wondered whether the parents were unable to engage with their children's experience, or did not think professional support was available or could be helpful.

Pacing

As with all family work, the first session began with introductions and putting the family at ease, before asking the children if they knew why we were meeting, and moving on to discuss what they were hoping we might address. Beginning with what children know and moving at their pace helps to ensure that we avoid introducing issues parents have not raised with them and issues that are out of synch with their preoccupations.

Where there is a wide age range it is important to try to present what is said in terms that are not too confusing for the youngest child, and if necessary, arrange another time to meet with the older children. As discussed in greater detail in the next chapter, where children are involved, it is also important to provide toys and drawing materials so that they are able to share and make sense of their concerns through play.

In this case, Sandra began by saying that they had come because their mother had cancer. Although each child had been told that Rachael had cancer, the questions they asked suggested a need to know more. As a result the session became a forum for the parents to help their children develop greater understanding of the probable course, prognosis and cause of the condition, correcting misunderstandings and discussing the importance of asking questions.

In explaining about cancer, Rachael and Andrew focused primarily on the concrete, on dates, measurements and factual information in what appeared to be an attempt to dispel the fears their children might have. Nonetheless, the hesitancies that marked much of what they said, and mismatch between the words they used and their non-verbal communication (for example, lack of eye contact) suggested that a great deal remained unsaid. Although it was important to respect parents' wishes to place a protective filter around their children, these hesitancies and mismatches suggested that some of what was not being said was too frightening and dangerous to share. With this in mind, although it was important to try to avoid interrupting the flow of what was said too often, the work included drawing attention to these hesitancies and mismatches with such phrases as 'I wonder why you decided not to finish that sentence?'

The panic and fear that had set in around the time of the diagnosis meant that in many ways the family were living in limbo. This sense of panic was reflected in the rapid way in which they talked and interrupted one another, and the inconsistencies that marked much of what was said. To reduce the sense of panic in the room, I mentioned my inability to think so quickly and concentrated on clarifying how frequently we could meet. This included recognizing the urgency of Rachael's concerns, as well as reminding the family that we could meet again. It was also helpful to discuss the actual process of the work, for example, asking 'Are we going too fast/slow?' and 'Are there issues you would like to address that we have not covered today?' (Burnham, 2005).

There also seemed to be a difference in the pace each person wanted to go, a difference that seemed to parallel the differences in their readiness to accept the inevitability of the progression of the disease. Rachael's insider position meant that she was desperate to avoid wasting time. In contrast, the rest of the family tended to hold back, possibly reflecting a hope that her condition might not change.

Later, it became apparent that she and Andrew had experienced considerable difficulties in their relationship before she became ill, which may have added to her urgency to try to create a different understanding before it was too late.

In some cases, there is a sudden deterioration in health. In these situations, it can be helpful for people to know that even though it has not been possible to resolve all the issues they had hoped to address, each person would be aware of their shared commitment to trying to establish a different relationship with one another.

Bringing less noticed aspects of experience to the fore

In a context that is organized around medical intervention, it is easy to forget the healing power of 'being there' (Meyerstein, 1994), of listening to the stories people tell, of sharing their pain, hopes and fears of abandonment and helping them reflect on what the experience of illness means for themselves and their loved ones.

However, as one story can never embrace all aspects of our experience, other stories are always possible. With this in mind, where people are struggling, the work includes introducing ideas, questions and comments that allow for a less pathologizing understanding of oneself and one's relationships with others. Uncovering these alternative stories requires a process of 'double listening': instead of only listening *to* stories with a view to gathering information or noting symptoms, we need to listen out *for* stories, for the stories that are absent but implicit in what is said (White and Epston, 1990; Weingarten, 1994). This involves listening to the ways in which people position themselves in the stories they tell, exploring the implications of the positions they adopt and drawing attention to exceptions to the problem-dominated story.

For example, some treat their experience of illness with enormous seriousness, while others use humour in what may be an attempt to deny or minimize the consequences of the illness, or oscillate between these two strategies. Being aware of these differences offers some guidance on how to ensure that what we say fits with the ways in which they conceptualize their experience. If the stories we hear are dominated by illness, it can be helpful to encourage people to reflect on other aspects of their lives (or vice versa). Similarly, where people's accounts of their experience are dominated by powerlessness and self-blame, it can be helpful to encourage them to reflect on times when they felt more able to address the challenges they faced.

This might include focus on the actual words people use. For example, Rachael used the metaphor of a drooping plant in describing how burdened her children were by her illness. This offered us a frame for discussing how she could help her children grow and thrive, despite the difficulties they were facing. Elsewhere, phrases like 'I would rather be seen dead than' and 'I'm sick to death' led to discussing how death seemed to creep into everyday conversations

As is often the case, there were times when pain and fatigue meant that Rachael's primary relationship seemed to be with the illness rather than her family (Mason, 2004). Although it is important to respect the demands illness presents, where this comes to dominate all aspects of their personal and family experience, it can be helpful to shift the focus to other aspects of their lives, as, for example, by using a technique White and Epston (1990) call 'externalization'. When problems have continued for some time, it is common to feel that the problem is beyond our control and an integral part of our character. The disempowerment and shame that tends to accompany problems that feel close to home tend to have a silencing and immobilizing effect, so that becomes particularly difficult to effect any change. Separating ourselves from the problem tends to relieve the pressure of blame and defensiveness.

With this in mind, the family was asked to imagine what cancer might look like. This resulted in describing cancer as a large ball that seemed to have rolled into the centre of their lives, taking over and leaving little space for anything else. No longer defined as the problem or under scrutiny, Rachael was able to assume a more reflective position in relation to the concerns she had. Seeing cancer as a ball rather than a description of who Rachael had become enabled the rest of the family to adopt a somewhat different position as well, so that it became more possible to ask questions and talk about other family needs without feeling as if they were being disrespectful of her position.

Another way of bringing alternative aspects of experience to the fore is by reframing what is said. At one point Rachael said she felt a failure because she found it difficult to answer her son's questions about the future. What her son's question revealed was that even though he knew this was a sensitive issue, he felt safe enough to ask her and was looking to her for help in making sense of his experience. Other possibilities include encouraging members of the family to imagine how they might see things if they were to swap places with one another, and in the case of parents who seem unable to connect with their children, to ask what was or would have been important to them as children faced with a similar situation.

Questions that open up alternative ways of thinking

Although questions can be used to gather new information, open-ended questions offer another useful way of extending, reframing or redefining people's views, of bringing the perceptions we have of one another into increased visibility, and where people's accounts of themselves are problem dominated, opening up discussions about their strengths. However, rather than interrogating people or positioning ourselves as experts, as suggested below, the questions we ask need to be part of a collaborative and non-judgemental conversation and based on a respectful sense of curiosity (Hoffman, 1993; Tomm, 1988).

This could involve asking people to imagine how someone sitting in the same room sees the issues under discussion. Although this form of 'gossiping' can feel strange, it provides a context for discussing and contesting the assumptions we have about one another. Similarly asking children and young people about their experience can increase parents' understanding of their position. Questions can also be used to introduce the idea that gender informs experience, as in asking:

- If you were a man (*or woman*), how might your response be different?
- How does being a girl (*or boy*) impact on people's expectations of what you need or should do?

It is also possible to open up discussions about the past by asking parents such as questions as:

- How do the concerns you are raising connect with experiences within your own childhood?
- How does the sort of care your children receive compare with the care you received?
- How does the support you would (or would not) want from others compare with the support you were able to give your own parents?

Where the accounts people present suggest change is impossible, questions offer a useful way of increasing people's awareness of the potential problems associated with their current life style, the consequences they are or are likely to experience, and risks faced as a result of the behaviour in question (Miller and Rollnick, 2002). Bringing discrepancies to the fore in this way opens up the possibility of shifting the focus to envisaging a better future and becoming increasingly motivated to achieve this change, as in:

- What worries you about your current situation?
- What makes you think you need to do something about your drinking, diet or level of exercise?
- How does this behaviour stop you from doing what you want to do in life?
- What do you see as the good things about giving up drugs or loosing weight?
- What makes you think that you could make these changes if you did decide to do so?
- Who could help you take this step?[1]

It is difficult to contemplate changing our behaviour if we feel we are not capable of this change. Where people seem to feel particularly powerless, asking questions that bring their strengths to the fore can shift the focus from powerlessness to confidence about the ability to adopt a different stance, as with such questions as:

- How did your son know he could turn to you for help in making sense of what your/his illness means?

- What personal strengths have helped you deal with difficult challenges in the past (*and/or could help you succeed in the present*)?
- Can you say what your child/partner/parent treasures about you?

Asking people to rate their confidence about responding differently on a scale of 1 to 10 opens up the possibility of discussing what is needed for them to feel more confident about the possibility of change. Rating questions are also helpful when there seems to be a taboo on acknowledging difference, as they introduce the idea that each person's view is unique and one person's response is not more correct than another:

- Who is most worried about mummy, who is second most worried, etc.?
- Who in the family tends to get angry most easily, who is second?

In contrast, where people's accounts are only about difference, including differences in health status, asking questions about other aspects of their lives can bring more of what is shared to the fore. The fear and uncertainty that surround situations of illness mean that it is not unusual for family relationships to become 'frozen' in the present. Focusing on the here-and-now and taking each day as it comes can be extremely valuable in situations of uncertainty. However, where this continues for a protracted period of time, people tend to become less able to deal flexibly with the challenges they are facing. As such, useful questions to ask include:

- How might you deal differently with the concerns you have about your daughter/son if you/your partner was not unwell?
- How might your expectations of your children be different in two years' time?
- What questions might your children ask as they get older?

Where the family seems to be stuck in survival mode after the crisis has abated it can also be helpful to encourage them to reflect on how aspects of their 'pre-illness' lives had given them a sense of strength and confidence before, and explore what needs to happen for them to engage with these aspects of their lives once more.

Challenging narratives of blame

Feelings of blame and guilt tend to have a profound effect on our ability to be there for one another. As discussed in Chapter 2, one of the most common responses to finding out we, or someone we love, is seriously ill or dying is to ask why. Often this means blaming ourselves or someone else for causing or exacerbating the illness. However, even though our actions and life style can affect certain aspects of health, the likelihood of contracting a life-limiting condition depends on a wide range of factors. Similarly, even if the disease is genetically transmitted, this does not imply intentionality.

As mentioned earlier, in some ways the family seemed to be living in limbo. With this in mind, when meeting Rachael and Andrew on their own I asked them about the earlier stages of the disease in order to understand what might making it more difficult for them to move on. What I learned was that Rachael became ill a short while after Lucy was born. Looking back, both parents, but Rachael in particular, said that they remembered very little about Lucy's early year as they had been preoccupied with fear about her health, with trying to ensure she received the best possible treatment, minimizing the extent to which the rest of their children's activities were disrupted, and coming to terms with the loss of the future they had imagined they would have with one another.

The practicalities of coping with the illness and guilt seemed to have meant that they had found it far more difficult to set realistic boundaries for Lucy, as had been possible with the rest of their children. As the work progressed, it also became apparent that the other reason it was more difficult to be consistent with Lucy was that had they known that Rachael was at risk of developing cancer, they would have terminated her last pregnancy.

As guilt seemed to be a dominant aspect of their relationship with Lucy, it was important to introduce thoughts and questions that might challenge these beliefs, as in:

- Acknowledging the presence of blame, for example by commenting on verbal and non-verbal cues that suggested they were blaming themselves and/or one another.
- Interrupting accounts of blame by exploring and introducing discrepancies in factual information.
- Exploring the impact of blame on relationships and the suffering it tends to bring.
- Reflecting on the emptiness of blame and its failure to avert the course of the condition.

Although it was important to avoid discrediting the reality of their experience, exploring the ways in which blame seemed to be affecting relationships within the family helped Rachael and Andrew shift their preoccupations to paying more attention to the sort of care Lucy needed in the present. It was important to explore exceptions to the 'rule' they had presented, times when they were able to discipline Lucy in what they felt was an appropriate way. For example, Rachael's responses to Lucy during the family sessions indicated that, even though she might not be able to do as much as she might have had she been stronger, her daughter listened to her when she spoke in an authoritative way.

The work also included exploring what support they needed from one another in order to be able to set more consistent boundaries. Like many couples, although Rachael and Andrew had a somewhat different approach to discipline, because Rachael had been the primary caregiver before, this had caused little difficulty. However, as Andrew assumed a greater role in childcare, these differences assumed greater importance. In addition, Rachael's guilt about being unable to offer what she thought her children needed meant that she seemed to find disagreements about parenting a challenge to her sense of competence as a mother and as a person. In contrast, Andrew's ambivalence about having to assume more responsibility for their children meant that he veered between taking over in a way that emphasized Rachael's powerlessness, retreating, and looking to her for advice.

Often it is people who have had the greatest control over their lives who experience the greatest self-blame and struggle most to give up control (Reiss et al., 1986). Rachael's fear about her condition, desire to hold on to her pre-illness identity and attempts to protect her family meant that she tried to underplay the extent of her disability. As a result, there were times when she took on more than she could manage, resulting in her becoming enormously tired and lashing out in anger.

Talking together, hearing and reflecting on their differences helped Rachael and Andrew confront their shared and individual losses, establish some form of hope, and plan for the future. This does not mean that they felt able to share all their worries with one another or that there were never times when they became angry and disappointed in one another or themselves. However, it helped them grieve for what they had lost and reframe aspects of their roles, increasing their tolerance for one another as well as for the ambiguous situation they were in, and to clarify what was still physically feasible for Rachael and plan around this.

Normalizing the disruptive impact of illness

Because ideas about family functioning tend to be developed on the basis of people whose lives are not dominated by illness, there are no acknowledged 'norms' to help people make sense of what is and is not usual when someone in the family has a life-limiting and debilitating condition. As such, sharing what we have learnt from the literature and previous clinical work can go a long way towards framing difficulties that feel like personal concerns or even failure, as part of a wider collective experience, as a 'normal' response to an 'abnormal' situation. This includes sharing that, despite their best intentions, many families find:

- The need to maximize the chances of healing can mean that the developmental, practical and emotional needs of the rest of the family are neglected.
- It can be difficult for those who are not ill to express their own concerns.
- The needs of the ill person that are unrelated to the illness tend to be ignored, increasing the extent to which their identity becomes subsumed by illness.
- Illness and disability can lead to shifts in patterns of power and dependency, creating a build up in tension that is difficult to address for fear of adding to the distress both parties face.
- Where a parent is ill, expectations of gendered roles may need to shift to ensure that they and the rest of the family receive the sort of care that is needed.
- Children seem to cope best when they are given information they can understand, can ask questions and are allowed to make sense of their own experience.

Rather than positioning myself as an expert, in discussing sharing this information, I tend to preface what I say with such comments as 'I am not sure if this is true for you, but something other parents/children have said or found helpful is ...'. This means that people are given this information but do not feel forced to act on it. For example, in working with this family, normalizing provided a frame for discussing some of the communication difficulties that had arisen. This included sharing that although parents often try to censor what they feel might be frightening for their children to take on board, children tend to pick up non-verbal cues. This means that instead of being protective, pretending nothing has changed can have the opposite effect, increasing rather than decreasing children's fear and confusion about the changes they see around them.

Normalizing was also a useful frame for discussing the escalation of tensions between Rachael and Sandra. As is often the case when a mother is ill, the oldest child Sandra had begun to assume a significant amount of responsibility for her two younger siblings. Although this had a largely positive impact on her sense of agency and self-esteem, acting in this way was not without problems. For example, stepping into what were effectively her mother's shoes meant that Sandra was at risk of being seen as accentuating her mother's disability. It also placed her in a different position to her siblings and meant that her preoccupations were very different from those of her peers. Framing these imbalances in power and alliances as a pattern that often develops in situations of parental illness helped her parents to think about how they could free Sandra to develop a life that was more in keeping with that of her peers.

However, it would have been impossible to encourage Sandra to stand back unless she was sure that someone else would take her place. As such, the work needed to include thinking about the possibility of her father or an outside helper assuming more responsibility for some of the tasks Sandra was expected (or expected herself) to fulfil. To affirm her position as a daughter and sibling rather than carer, she and her brother Pete were invited to a session in which they were able to raise issues that were particular to their positions as the older two children.

Reworking family boundaries

Amongst the consequences of being seriously ill is that the affected person may have far less control over their own body. However, it can also mean that the rest of the family have less control over certain aspects of their lives than before, including the boundary they might otherwise have maintained between themselves and the outside world.

This became apparent in a session in which Rachael discussed her embarrassment about the way her son Pete had behaved towards one of the care workers who came to help her wash and dress. In discussing this further, it became apparent his behaviour was partly an expression of the anger, frustration and fears that he and others had about the fact that his mother was ill.

Although Pete and his siblings resented these outsiders and thought they could manage without them, Rachael felt that it was preferable to relying even more on her family. She was also afraid of asking Andrew to assume more of the burden of caring for her. Nonetheless, she resented the fact that he and their children seemed happy to stand back and leave her to the care of others. Discussions about the practicalities of their everyday lives revealed that the care workers tended to be around at times that felt particularly intrusive, at the start and the end of the day. This led to exploring whether it might be possible to restructure the package of care in any way and inviting the care worker in question to attend one session to help her gain a greater understanding about their family. Although it was impossible to re-create the sort of privacy they might have had if Rachael had been well, these discussions helped Pete and the rest of the family to feel that their needs and wishes had been taken seriously.

Disentangling illness from who one 'really' is

As some of the difficulties associated with parenting were bound up with difficulties between Rachael and Andrew, the work included sessions with them on their own. Stories about their earlier relationship suggested that they had been drawn to one another by physical attraction and a shared love of sport. However, Rachael's illness had placed considerable restrictions on the physical pleasure they could give and receive. She was far less mobile. Rachael tended to deal with this by withdrawing and becoming tearful, and Andrew by increasing his commitment to remaining physically fit.

Although it was important to tread carefully in exploring an issue that was clearly very painful to both of them, some acknowledgement of shared and different loss was crucial to enabling Rachael and Andrew to expose their vulnerability to one another and reflect on what they might want or could ask for in the present. This included trying to disentangle the illness and aftermath of treatment from who Rachael 'really' was in the present and from other aspects of their relationship. As in working with other couples where much of what they said was presented in polarized terms, the questions and ideas I raised were aimed at exploring what might be shared. This allowed for an acknowledgement that Rachael was not only a recipient of care, but remained an important source of nurturance for Andrew as well as their children.

Few of us are able to tolerate unrelenting exposure to loss, and we need to retain beliefs that maximize coping and adaptation. Exploring what they had learned about themselves and each other over the course of the illness helped in shifting the focus away from what seemed to be spiralling loss. Similarly, talking about the importance of maintaining precious rituals like birthday celebrations and certain religious traditions helped in placing some limits on the potentially all-embracing nature of their loss, providing a concrete confirmation and consolidation of relationships.

Linking the present and the past

The emotional turmoil surrounding experiences of illness can result in bringing aspects of experience together in a different way, creating an opportunity to resolve issues that relate to the past and establish a more comfortable understanding of oneself and relationships with others. This is not always the case: where relationships are particularly troubled, feelings of guilt, regret, shame and blame can become so pervasive that they limit people's opportunity to make use of the time they have together.

As the work progressed, it became apparent that prior marital disharmony and fears of abandonment limited Rachael and Andrew's availability to one another. Although the past is not prescriptive of how we respond in the present, reflecting on the links between the present and past led to recognizing that feelings of being treated with disdain in the present were informed by situations in which they had felt devalued by one another in the past.

However, responses to illness in the present are also informed by family histories of illness, loss and disempowerment. Byng-Hall (1995) proposed that although family histories and the stories that are told about the past do not determine the ways in which we respond to the present, they become the 'family scripts' or internalized templates we draw on in reaching decisions about the present.

Whilst some of us seem to focus our energy on trying to replicate the past, others focus more on trying to avoid replicating aspects of the past we found intolerable and inappropriate when we were younger. However, at times of emotional intensity it is not uncommon to be drawn back in to replicating internalized patterns of relating we had sought to escape. Similarly, even if we try to replicate the patterns of the past, we are different from our parents, and the situations we face are different: as such, this is never possible.

Genograms (or family trees) are a useful way of tracing these histories. Medical professionals will be familiar with genograms as they tend to be used in trying to establish the aetiology of disease, or to help people understand their risks of contracting a certain condition. In medical contexts, this involves asking the ill person or, in the case of children, a parent, questions about their family history of disease and life style choices that might affect health. Where people cannot answer these questions they may ask their relatives for help in filling in the gaps. However, relatives may be uncomfortable about sharing certain sorts of information. They are unlikely to have been told about diseases that occurred when they were younger. Medical genograms can be particularly challenging when someone has been adopted: although the adoptive family may be able to provide some information or gather additional information from adoption agency records, what is known tends to be limited.

Genograms are also a powerful therapeutic tool. Talking about who the members of one's family are and recording major life-changing events, offers a vehicle for sharing and tracing the ways in which certain beliefs and experiences have been transmitted across the generations and offers a way of making sense of the impact of the past on the present. It enables families to share their ideas, thoughts and feelings in a very different way, and can result in members of the family disclosing stories they have not shared before (Adam, 2009; McGoldrick et al., 1999).

The format I tend to use involves establishing the names and ages of as many family members as possible and dates of events like birth, marriage, divorce, separation and death of three or more generations (see Appendix 1). I also tend to ask if people want to include anyone else, for example a special friend or pet animal, as well as noting predictable and unpredictable events such as changes in the life course, in occupation, location and experiences of illness. Lines, boxes, circles and symbols are used to depict interactions that span three or more generations. As illness can result in an imbalance in care, it can be helpful to use arrows to depict the main directions of care across the generations. Where migration and cultural or religious difference is a central feature of people's experience, it can be useful to denote this as well.

Using a large sheet of paper enables family members to work on their genogram together. This can be kept aside and added to over the course of the work. However, discussions about the past are only effective when they are linked with the concerns the people are facing. In the context of illness, this means paying particular attention to the ways in which stories of loss, separation and care have been transmitted across the generations.

The diagnosis of Rachael's illness confronted the family with powerful feelings of sadness, anger, guilt, disappointment, separation anxiety and desperation. Talking about her own parents, Rachael said that although her mother had not been ill, she saw her as powerless and felt that her father had treated her mother in a dismissive way. As such, she had been determined to avoid finding herself in a similar position.

In contrast, Andrew's mother had been disabled for much of his life, placing what he felt were unrealistic demands on him as well as his father. In marrying someone who appeared to be strong and like him, who placed a high value on fitness, he had hoped to avoid finding himself in this position as an adult. In both cases, there were other legacies of loss as well: at least one of their grandparents had left their country of birth to escape anti-Semitism, and had never seen their non-migrant parents again. These conversations helped them to grieve for what had been lost, including the fact that Rachael might not be able to see her children become adults and parents themselves.

When the condition is terminal

Some time after this work ended, Rachael called to say that she had become increasingly unwell and that she and Andrew needed help in planning for the future. On meeting with them, the parents said that they were particularly worried about Lucy: she seemed frightened of being left alone with her mother and had become increasingly preoccupied with her father's health. In reflecting on what might underlie her preoccupation, they realized that even though she had not been told that her mother's condition had deteriorated, she had sensed this and had become afraid of losing her father as well. This led to a decision to raise an issue they had been afraid of discussing with their children before: who would take care of them in the event neither parent was there.

Where the condition is terminal, helping the family prepare for the future while the ill person is able to participate helps to alleviate the likelihood of the survivors basing their lives according to the desires and injunctions they imagine the dying person would have had, enabling them to get on with their lives in the knowledge that they have the blessing of the deceased.

In this case, the television screening of a programme about euthanasia provided the impetus for Rachael to share her end of life plans and ask Andrew to ensure that her life would not be prolonged beyond a point when it was no longer meaningful. Final requests can have great power: where relationships have been particularly troubled, they may assist the dying and surviving to achieve some resolution (Pipher, 1999). However, they can also put the rest of the family in a 'double bind' (Bateson, 1972), particularly when these wishes are not shared and have problematic legal implications.

As discussed in greater detail in Chapter 8, in these situations, it is important to ensure that families have space for careful discussion, are offered non-intrusive, non-judgemental support and are given the information they require on which to base their decision (Montalvo et al., 1998). However, tensions can easily escalate, particularly when it is difficult to know what the terminally ill person would want.

Although much of what has been said here focuses on interpersonal relationships, there are times when we need to grapple with the challenges we face on our own. At no time is this more crucial than when the end is near. In this case, there were times when Rachael and Andrew needed to think through their experiences alone, and others when being alone seemed to compound the fear and loneliness they were experiencing.

Moreover, as helpful as any of the techniques outlined here may be, what is probably most important is the capacity to 'be there' at times of distress. For people to trust us with their most private struggles, they need to feel that we (be this a professional, or a member of the family) have a sense of integrity, that we are ready and not too embarrassed or too judgemental to understand what they are facing, be this fear of death, envy of others' health or irritation with well-meaning comments about courage, that we are able to acknowledge what we cannot know and are touched by their experience without being overwhelmed.

Summary

- A systemic approach places primary emphasis on interactions in the here-and-now, on the interactions that appear to have created or are maintaining that problem.
- However, as past experiences can have a profound effect on the present, it also involves exploring the link between the present and past.
- Where someone is seriously ill, disabled or dying, the work involves:
  o Establishing a context in which people feel able to express their concerns without being discrediting or having to defend their position
  o Holding at least two dimensions in mind: the illness and aspects that relate to the rest of their lives
  o Respecting the individual and family's resources and sense of authority

- o Listening to what people say as well as listening out for what is absent but implicit.
- Where much of what is said focuses on differences, it is important to explore what might be shared (*and the reverse when differences are not acknowledged*).
- Similarly, when most of what is said focuses on illness with little reference to other aspects of experience, the work includes bringing other aspects of experience to the fore (*and the reverse when illness-related concerns are not acknowledged*).

4

CHILDHOOD AND ADOLESCENT EXPERIENCES OF ILLNESS

A significant body of research suggests that children[1] who have had a life-limiting illness or whose siblings or parents have been seriously ill show higher levels of emotional and behavioural problems than the norm, and for a period of time become hyper-alert to signs of danger, and/or experience difficulties in concentrating and memory problems. This is not necessarily the case: other studies suggest that it is difficult to distinguish these groups of children, or that they perform better than the norm (Noll and Kupt, 2007; Romer et al., 2002). Indeed, as when faced with other adverse and potentially traumatic situations, research and clinical experience suggests that children are less likely to develop long-term problems when they are able to turn to someone who can hold their needs in mind, when they experience a sense of agency and where the family is supportive, optimistic and communicates openly.

Age and understanding

Children's experience and understanding of illness is informed by their age. For example, knowing how old the child was when they, a sibling or parent was diagnosed gives some indication of their ability to process what they see and hear, and differentiate between their parent's body and their own. In addition, age also tends to inform what children are told, whether or not parents had an opportunity to establish confidence in their parenting capacity before the illness developed, and where a parent or sibling is ill, expectations about the roles they should play in relation to household chores and caring for others in their parents' absence.

Studies of early development suggest that infants and young children come to know themselves through the experience of being recognized by a primary caregiver, and that this relationship is central to subsequent psychological wellbeing (Bowlby, 1953; Stern, 1985). As infants will not have developed the capacity to differentiate themselves from their parent, being separated from their parents (including at times of illness) can be deeply disturbing, giving rise to what has been called 'separation anxiety'. Even though infants and young children are not able to put their experiences of these times into words, they are encoded in the form of emotional, sensory and visceral memory and can come to the fore when faced with subsequent experiences of separation.

Increased recognition of the potentially harmful consequences of early separation has led to initiatives aimed at shortening children's stay in hospital, offering parents less restricted visiting hours and a chance to room-in with hospitalized children, minimizing the number of professionals involved in their care. Where separation is unavoidable, parents are encouraged to prepare their children and ensure that the people caring for them in their absence understand their unique needs, such as which teddy they like to take to bed.

As they become toddlers and pre-schoolers, children develop a greater awareness of what is happening around them. When they are given no explanation for what is happening, they tend to develop their own, which can include understanding that the separation (or illness) is a punishment for bad behaviour. The belief that the illness can be caused by 'bad' thoughts or behaviours means that it is not unusual for young children to think that it is wrong to be happy, and try to bargain with fate, for example by promising to be good (Romer et al., 2002). Because they tend to have less understanding of where the boundaries between themselves and others are, young children may be unsure whether the illness (or badness) is located inside or outside their own body, which may account for why it is not unusual for them to regress in what appears to be an attempt to return to a time when life felt safer (Judd, 1989). Where the person who is ill is a sibling or parent, children often make sense of what is happening by copying what they see: although 4-year-old Tommy did not know his mother had developed secondaries in her bones, he had started to limp, mimicking her altered gait.

Adolescents express themselves and experience illness somewhat differently. Factors such as rapid brain development, the pressures of secondary education, increasingly complex family and peer relationships and growing awareness of sexuality mean that adolescents tend to be more reactive to stress and develop greater difficulties in self-regulation around this time of life (Dahl, 2004; Shore, 2001). However, there seem to be differences between younger and later adolescence. The ages of twelve and fifteen tend to be characterized by the acquisition of formal logical thought, onset of biological sexuality, growth of the physical structure, entering into mixed gendered groups and challenging adult rules and expectations. In contrast, from fifteen onwards adolescents tend to reach physical maturity, seek greater intimacy with the opposite sex, acquire adult skills, clarify their values and rework patterns of connection with family, with many continuing to work out issues of sexuality, intimacy and independence into their twenties.

Particularly in the west, most young people become increasingly independent and take more risks as they move through adolescence. However, this is less feasible when one is seriously ill or becomes physically and/or cognitively impaired as a result of an accident. For example, unlike their peers, adolescents with chronic conditions like diabetes, Crohn's disease and ulcerative colitis have to be careful about what they eat and drink to avoid the possibility of a flare up in their condition (Helgeson and Novak, 2006). Where life starts to feel too constrained, non-adherence may be the only way of asserting themselves. However, instead of increasing the possibilities of being more independent it keeps worries about health at the forefront of their doctors', parents' and their own minds. As such, it is important to find arenas for self-assertion that are less risky to health and ways in which adherence does not compromise their lives and the lives of the rest of the family more than necessary.

Fitting in with peers tends to become more important during adolescence as well. Where illness has resulted in temporary or permanent disfigurement or reliance on aids like a catheter, it may be possible to hide this by the clothes one wears. Despite this, many continue to be preoccupied with an internalized sense of difference even if this is no longer visible. Concerns about fitting in also mean that some adolescents become more embarrassed about being seen with someone who is physically disabled, or about interacting with someone whose speech is severely slurred, giving rise to feelings of shame and regret that are difficult to acknowledge.

One of the other challenges they and their families face is that young people with a chronic condition are usually transferred from paediatrics to adult services care at some point in their adolescence. This can be enormously beneficial because it allows adolescents to assume a level of responsibility that is more in keeping with that of their peers. As a heightened sense of vulnerability means that many young people (and indeed their parents) are not ready for this transfer, it is important to prepare them for this step (Bloomquist et al., 1998). However, because professionals who work with adults are not necessarily equipped or may not feel able to deal with the challenges and preoccupations of this age group, several units have begun to set aside clinic times that are particular to adolescents. This has the advantage of offering young people a chance to meet others in a similar position on an informal basis. Some clinics have also started to run groups for adolescents. As a high proportion of people with HIV/AIDs in sub-Saharan Africa are adolescents, one of the additional benefits of group sessions is that they are an opportunity to share dilemmas unaffected peers will have little understanding of, such as how and when to disclose their status to a potential sexual partner (PATA, 2010).

Age-related experiences of risk taking and independence are also likely to be less feasible when a parent or sibling is seriously ill, partly because adolescents tend to be expected to assume additional responsibility for household chores and supporting other family members when parents are less able to perform these tasks. This is particularly true of girls, regardless of their age. Although these tasks can be extremely burdensome, they offer the young person an opportunity to experience the sense of agency and emotional connection that arises from being able to help and to be recognized as supportive at a time when so much of their life feels beyond their control. Whilst boys tend to be freer to engage in their usual activities, they are likely to have fewer opportunities to participate and experience themselves as supportive (Eiser, 1997).

Gilligan (1982) and Frosh et al.'s (2002) studies of gendered identity offer insight into the somewhat different challenges adolescent girls and boys are likely to face. Gilligan found that instead of viewing morality in terms of the universal external set of principles, girls tend to view care and interpersonal relationships as deciding factors in resolving moral dilemmas and interpersonal conflicts. This suggests that prioritizing one's one needs when others are in difficulty will be more complicated for girls than boys. In contrast, Frosh et al. found that acting in ways that are at odds with society's images of masculinity (as, for example, showing feelings and talking about relationships) increases the likelihood of being mocked by one's friends. It is therefore hardly surprising that one of the greatest fears of 13-year-old Stephen about returning to school after his father died was of crying in front of his friends.

Research provides inconsistent data on the extent to which age influences the development of long-term problems: some studies suggest that younger children are at greater risk because they are more reliant on their primary caretaker, while others suggest that because younger children are less able to understand what is happening they are more protected (Last et al., 2005). Moreover, age-related differences may not relate to differences in levels of comprehension but to the fact that older children tend to be told more, receive less support and are usually expected to assume a larger role in supporting those who are younger (Armsden and Lewis, 1994; Thastum et al., 2008).

Verbal and non-verbal communication

As young children tend to make sense of their experience by what they see and hear, in trying to help them understand what is happening it is important to focus on the concrete and visible, as in using drawings or a toy to locate the illness and discuss what the treatment will entail. For example, Ramona explained to her 3-year-old daughter Judy that she had cancer by asking her to touch the 'little lumps' (tumours) on her neck. However, misunderstandings easily arise: at a later point, Judy said the lumps on her mother's neck were caused by 'lettuce in a lump'. This left her mother puzzled until she remembered choking on lettuce some time before.

Older children benefit from being given more abstract and scientific information. This helps them create some sense of control in a situation that tends to feel beyond control. However, regardless of their age, parents and professionals rarely refer to the fears and worries they and the child may have. As a result, although 11-year-old Peter was able to discuss the development of his mother's cancer in terms of red and white blood cells, his scientific understanding was unable to protect him from the fears he had, as reflected in a repetitive nightmare about a monster taking over his body.

Where there is a lack of fit between what children see and hear, they tend to develop their own understanding, and their drawings and imaginative play often suggest a preoccupation with health and worries about bodily mutilation even if they do not 'know' someone is ill (Gabriels et al., 2000). Indeed, there seem to be at least three levels of knowing: a *knowing that*, a theoretical or descriptive knowledge that implies a taking in of, or clarification of information; a *knowing how*, a practical knowing that involves method and skill; and a *relational knowing*, a knowing that is held in common and need not be put into words (Shotter, 1994).

There are obviously many situations where parents might want to filter what children are told and process what they have heard before sharing this with their children. Although it is important to respect parents' views, it is also important for them to know that research and clinical experience indicates that when children are given information they can understand and are kept up to date with changes in the illness and treatment, those who are ill experience less depression, siblings of ill children display increased social competence and when a parent is ill, there is less of a tendency for magical thinking (Davey et al., 2003; Romer et al., 2002). Although there is no best way of sharing information that is likely to be distressing, it is preferable to:

- Stay as close to the truth possible.
- Explain what is happening in a way that fits with children's level of understanding.
- Use drawings to illustrate what the illness and treatment entail.
- Treat children with respect.
- Reassure them they are not responsible for the cause or course of the condition.
- Offer suggestions of other ways of helping that are manageable.

Ideally, discussions about illness should take place in an environment in which children are not exposed to unnecessary anxiety-evoking stimuli or interruptions, and where it is possible to hear, be heard and if need be cry in privacy. As with people of all ages, children's responses to worrying circumstances vary: while some try to find out as much as possible, others tend to suppress information that seems too threatening (Miller, 1995). Similarly, although it is best to follow the child's pace, some children need their parents' blessing before being able to voice their own concerns.

Childhood illness

Although there are many overlaps with situations in which a sibling or parent has a life-limiting illness, being diagnosed with a serious illness tends to set ill children apart from their siblings and age-mates. To date, studies of the psychological consequences of childhood illness have yielded conflicting results. Some suggest that children are likely to be left with long-term difficulties, and that even if they are cured tend to develop a heightened sense of vulnerability. Others suggest that provided children are well supported, they are able to adjust and lead relatively anxiety-free lives (Campbell, 2003). Nonetheless, there is a general consensus that children cope best when there is:

- No recurrence of the disease.
- A short course of treatment.
- Early diagnosis.
- A generally optimistic outlook on life prior to the onset of illness.
- A family that is supportive and able to communicate openly.

In trying to make sense of children's experience, it can be difficult to separate responses that relate to the physical from those that relate to the psychological. For example, acting in a 'grumpy' way after a kidney or bone marrow transplant may relate to the side effects of drugs the child is required to take to minimize rejection. It may also be a psychological response to this potentially life-changing experience and to issues that are quite unrelated to health. However, the significance of parent–child relationships to each party means that children's experience of illness is also likely to be bound up with the ways in which their parents feel and respond. Gender also appears to play a role. For example, Hill and Zimmerman (1995) found that mothers of children with sickle cell disease see their sons as sicker than daughters and are more restrictive of their activity, regardless of physiological severity. In contrast, other research suggests that girls perceive their parents as more supportive of their being ill, tend to receive more sympathy and are allowed more relief from other responsibilities when ill than is the case for boys, and that mothers tend to be more encouraging of illness-related behaviour than fathers (Walker and Zeman, 1992).

Case example

Alex, an 11-year-old boy with end-stage renal failure, was referred to the psycho-social liaison team as there were concerns about his poor adherence with the treatment.

On meeting with the family, Alex's mother Petra began by detailing her frustrated attempts to persuade her son to follow the treatment regime more closely. Alex responded by expressing his frustration with his mother, and in particular with her acting as if she 'owned' his body. Petra defended herself by recounting the many times when Alex had put himself at increased risk, resulting in a significant deterioration in health. Although his father Jim had tried to encourage Petra to step back, she could not take this on board because she felt he did not take his own health problems (high blood pressure) seriously enough. However, it is also possible that one of the difficulties of stepping back was that it would have meant relinquishing a role that had become central to how she saw herself.

Although all three of them found the current situation intolerable, they seemed unable to hear one another's concerns and suggestions or imagine acting differently. With this in mind, the work involved trying to help them to hear one another more, increase their curiosity and understanding of one another's position, normalize some of the challenges they were facing and ask questions aimed at introducing different ways of thinking, as in asking Alex:

- What worries do you have about your health?
- How is your condition restricting your life?
- What would have to happen for your parents to trust you to assume more responsibility for your own care?
- How would your parents know when you are ready to take this on?

The work also included asking his parents how their treatment of Alex related to the amount of independence they had at this time of life and exploring experiences of illness in their own families. Recognizing that fears from their own earlier experiences were impacting on the present seemed to free the parents to hear one another and work together to help their son deal with the challenges he was facing.

When a brother or sister is seriously ill

Until recently, very little academic or clinical attention was paid to the positions of siblings of ill and severely disabled children. This is not particular to illness but indicative of the way in which the wider psychological literature has tended to neglect siblings. This seems to be shifting, as reflected in the growing number of studies demonstrating the profound impact of sibling relationships on experiences of self and relationships with others throughout our lives (Edwards et al., 2006; Mitchell, 2003).

The shared identification and companionship these relationships offer means that a brother or sister's illness can represent a profound threat to the healthy child's own sense of security. In discussing sibling relationships, Mitchell (2003) argues that our siblings are the people who at one level are most like us, but at another stand in our place. This suggests that a sibling's illness may signify the actualization of a child's fantasy of being able to supplant her or him in one's parents' eyes. However, it also suggests that that serious illness in a brother or sister can represent a threat to the healthy child's own sense of security.

Here too, research findings vary considerably. Some studies suggest that problems like social withdrawal, high levels of anxiety and jealousy, enuresis and academic underachievement are more pronounced amongst this group of children, and that levels of anxiety and low self esteem may mirror or even surpass that of their ill sibling. Other studies suggest that siblings who feel supported do not develop more problems than the norm, and that living with an ill sibling can result in an increased sense of compassion and sensitivity towards others (O'Brien et al., 2009; Sharpe and Rossiter, 2002). Despite these differences, siblings tend to cope best if they have:

- Access to someone who can hold their needs in mind.
- Opportunities that enhance their sense of self-worth.
- Help in mediating the guilt induced by being healthy.
- Daily routines that are maintained as much as possible.
- Recognition of their input.

Nonetheless, it is important to recognize the very real challenges growing up with a seriously ill or disabled sibling can present. For example, siblings are more likely to be faced with untimely and unexplained separation from parents, disruptions to daily routines and greater worries about their own health. In these situations, being competitive and successful can be experienced as emphasizing the differences in their health status, particularly where this relates to aspects of experience that are no longer open to their ill and/or disabled sister or brother, giving rise to what has been called 'survivor guilt'. Although the term was originally coined to describe the guilt of Holocaust survivors, it is being used more widely in relation to other situations to describe feelings of unworthiness in relation to those whose lives have been damaged, and relief about escaping a similar fate.

Case example

Returning to Alex and his family, because the hospital was a long way from home, Alex's only sibling (his twin brother Jack) was not invited to the initial family sessions. Over the course of the work it became apparent Jack was often reluctant to go to school and had been taken to their local hospital on several occasions with injuries that were the result of taking reckless risks while riding his bike. As such, Jack was included in some of the subsequent sessions.

In asking Jack and his family about their lives before Alex became ill, what emerged was that he and Alex had been extremely close, but that this had changed as Alex became increasingly ill. A number of factors seemed to contribute to this, including their parents' worries about Alex, his mother's need to accompany Alex to medical appointments and, because his father worked long hours, the fact that Jack was often left in the care of neighbours and friends. Although his parents tended to underplay the seriousness of Alex's condition, whispered conversations suggested the opposite, leaving Jack unsure whether he could trust what he was told. Indeed he tended to hear more from Alex than from his parents. However, the difficulty was that whilst Alex understood what he had been told, he found it difficult to explain this to Jack.

Discussions about the illness indicated that Jack felt he was to blame and felt guilty about his earlier jealousy of his brother, who had done much better than he had at school. Although it was important to affirm the reality of how he felt and normalize these fears, what was probably most helpful was hearing his brother say it was not his fault and that he was relieved that it was he rather than Jack who was ill. Whilst this interchange horrified their parents, it sensitized them to the challenges Jack was facing and the importance of their sons' relationship to them both.

Here too, questions helped to introduce a different perspective. For example, asking how life would be different if magically they woke to find that Alex was no longer ill opened up a discussion about the boys' shared and different areas of interest and competence, helping to separate other aspects of their relationship from the differences in their health. As parents' experiences of sibling relationships inform the ways in which they help their children make sense of their differences, it was important to encourage them to think about these relationships. In view of the difficulties Jack was having at school, it was also important to explore the possibility of receiving additional support from school.

When a parent is seriously ill

As with siblings, until recently relatively little attention was paid to the impact of parental illness on children's emotional wellbeing. This is starting to shift, as reflected in the growing numbers of research and clinical studies aimed at identifying the factors that help in minimizing the difficulties children face when a parent is physically ill (Altschuler and Dale, 1999; Thastum et al., 2008).

Many studies suggest there is a higher prevalence of problems amongst children whose parents are ill, particularly adolescent girls and boys between 6 and 12 (Armsden and Lewis, 1994; Visser et al., 2005).

Others suggest children function in similar or even better ways than norm groups (Hoke, 2001; Welch et al., 1996). In addition, although some studies have found that distress levels are greater when the prognosis is poorer and the duration of the disease is longer, others have found that subjective perceptions are more predictive of distress than objective characteristics. For example, children whose energies focus on dealing with the emotions evoked by parental illness tend to experience higher levels of distress than those who focus more on trying to do something about the actual illness or situation their parents are in (Compass et al., 1994; Visser et al., 2005). Here too, gender is important to bear in mind: some studies have found that children (particularly girls) show more symptoms when they are the same gender as the ill parent. However, this may reflect not actual differences in distress but gendered differences in expressing distress (Davey et al., 2003).

A large-scale analysis of the responses of children from 6 to late adolescence found that the concerns of younger children tend to revolve around guilt, worry about the possibility of a parent dying and fears of becoming ill themselves. Although adolescents expressed similar worries, they also tended to be concerned about having to assume additional levels of responsibility. Regardless of age, where the relationship was particularly conflicted before, there is a greater risk of children viewing the illness as the realization of an angry impulse (Christ et al., 1994; Romer et al., 2002). Nonetheless, children appear to fair better when:

- They are informed about the illness in a way they can understand.
- They continue to be cared for by their main caregiver.
- They do not have to suppress their own needs and are able to maintain important age-appropriate activities.
- They are able to turn to someone they can trust.
- They have some understanding of plans for the future.
- They know what to do, who to call at moments of crisis, and that older children have some knowledge of first aid.

Case example

Felicia contacted a child and family mental health clinic on finding out that, having been successfully treated for cancer about two years before, the cancer had returned. She suspected her 4-year-old daughter Sasha knew something was wrong as she had become increasingly unsettled and refused to sleep in her own bed. However, because she felt Sasha was particularly vulnerable, she was afraid of telling her about this recent diagnosis.

Fairly soon after starting the first session with Felicia, her partner James and Sasha, Sasha picked up a doll and pulled its legs off before driving a toy car around the room making loud siren sounds. Although I was keen to avoid going too fast, I asked Sasha where her car was going. Her answer was that the car was taking the doll to the hospital because she was very sick. This gave her mother the confidence to engage with what her daughter seemed to be saying, and she went on to tell her that, like the doll, she was sick.

Sasha responded by putting her arms around her mother. As this suggested a desire for comfort as well as a desire to protect her from the illness and possibly from the feelings her mother's illness had evoked in her, I wondered aloud whether she was trying to show that she was able to look after her mummy. This led to a discussion about the sort of help a child of her age could offer and the help her mummy would get from her daddy, the doctors and other grown ups. However, it also became apparent that some of Sasha's distress was a response to other changes in her life, including disruptions to her daily routine, leading to a discussion of whether they were able to draw on the support of anyone else to help her maintain as much of her usual routine as possible.

Working with children at times of particular difficulty

As with all work with illness, in working with children and their families, it is important to listen carefully, bear witness to the distress they are experiencing, and help them reflect on their shared and individual experiences by introducing ideas, suggestions and questions that allow for a different approach to the struggles they are having.

This means creating an environment in which children feel listened to rather than judged, where it is possible to communicate through play rather than having to rely purely on words, and where the focus is not only on troubles. Having play materials on hand, for example dolls, toy animals, puppets, soft objects like a teddy bear, and drawing materials, helps to reduce the fear and anxiety that tends to be associated with doctors and hospitals. As importantly, having play materials at hand means that it is possible to engage with some of the thoughts and fantasies they express through their play.

Drawing materials are particularly helpful as they can be used to explain where the illness is located and how it developed, and to ask questions about what they are told. Where children and their parents seem stuck in crisis mode, asking children to draw a 'before and after' picture of their home opens up the possibility of talking about what needs to happen before they feel ready or are allowed to resume aspects of their pre-illness lives. The powerlessness and shame that tend to surround problems that feel close to home mean that it can be difficult to separate oneself from the illness and its consequences. With this in mind, it can be helpful to externalize or objectify the illness and/or its consequences. This could involve asking the child (and/or the rest of their family) to name the problem, drawing it and speculating about its characteristics and motives.

This process is reflected in White and Epston's (1990) description of their work with a boy who had started to soil himself. Naming encopresis 'sneaky poo' enabled the family to talk about the problem as if it lay outside of this child, and helped him and his family engage with the problem in a more playful way. Discussing how the 'sneaky poo', an invisible entity, seemed to sneak up unawares and make him soil his pants helped to reduce the powerlessness and shame this young boy and his parents felt, enabling them to work together to reduce the likelihood of the problem recurring.

As suggested above, it is often preferable to address the concerns children have at one step removed. For example, Fredman et al. (2007) used a toy bear in working with a 10-year-old girl who was refusing to have any more surgery. As she would not explain to her parents or medical team why she was refusing surgery, she was asked if she would allow a teddy bear to express her views and let the therapists know when the bear got things wrong. Listening to the bear and commenting on what 'it' said helped to keep her engaged as well as helping her parents hear her. This led to the recognition that their daughter was not actually refusing surgery, and wanted her parents to know how difficult the thought of having to undergo more surgery was for her.

Another way of helping children and parents communicate about issues that are troubling is by asking members of the family to choose an animal counterpart to represent themselves and others, and using these images to construct a story (Arad, 2002). Although children and parents are not asked to focus on illness, their stories tend to reflect illness-related preoccupations. However, as reflected above, discussions about what is said need to begin with the animals in the stories before moving on to the people they might represent.

Activity sheets offer another way of helping children make sense of their experience, as in asking children to write or draw in response to activity sheets headed with such statements as 'who is in my family' and 'things that makes me sad/happy', columns marked 'life at home before (or after) X became ill' and diagrams of faces, animals, or what has been called a 'jelly bean tree': this is a sheet of paper with jelly bean characters depicting different sorts of emotions and connections to others, including characters sitting at the top or bottom, climbing up, and hanging on by their fingernails. Where children seem unable to draw on the strength their cultural heritage could offer, drawing a 'tree of life' that traces all aspects of their heritage offers a way of speaking about their cultural roots, skills, and the special people who live elsewhere.

Although the worksheets mentioned above are available on the net and in books, there may be times when it is more helpful to design something with the particular needs of that child in mind. As play offers children an opportunity to work through their own experience, opportunities for less structured play can be extremely helpful as well. However, even if children are seen on their own, it is important to help parents connect with their children's experience and regain or establish trust in their own capacity to be there for their children, rather than being drawn into acting like the 'better parent'. It is also important to recognize that there may be times when instead of empathizing, we find the child's behaviour irritating, aggressive and difficult to manage.

Group work

Group work offers children who have been exposed to life-limiting illness an opportunity to make sense of their experience in a context in which they are less exposed to reactions that hinder relationships in other situations, such as teasing. It helps to reframe thoughts and feelings that are understood to be personal as an almost inevitable response to the very unusual situation they face (Lobato and Kao, 2002; Williams et al., 2003).

While it is more usual to offer children who have been ill themselves the chance of participating in a group, several large-scale studies indicate that group work, particularly where it includes a psychoeducational element, is an effective way of helping children with an ill parent or sibling develop a better understanding of the disease, leading to improvements in general mood and a decline in behaviour problems (Kazak et al., 2005).

Children and adolescents tend to fair better when parents are offered a similar space to share their experiences with other parents. Meeting people who are in a similar position can help parents reframe thoughts, feelings and struggles which seem shameful as a 'normal' response to an extremely challenging position, enabling them to adopt more of an observer position and disentangle their own distress from that of the children (Goldstein and Friend, 2009). However, it can also be helpful to offer several families an opportunity to meet as a group, and move between sessions for the whole family and those in which children and parents meet on their own (Steinglass, 1998). Similarly, although group work is usually linked with the treatment unit, it is also possible to run groups in a setting that is unrelated (Olsson et al., 2005; Schmitt et al., 2007). Group work can also be used to familiarize children with the hospital prior to admission, as in using a doll or toy bear to simulate the procedures they are due to undergo.

Although some groups meet for one or two half-day sessions followed with another session at a later date, more usually this work takes place on a weekly or fortnightly basis for a predetermined amount of time. Whilst it is helpful to develop a provisional programme for each session, it is important to be able to respond flexibly to the issues that arise. For example, although the aim might be to focus on illness-related concerns, very often children's role-plays, stories and art work reflect concerns about other aspects of their lives, such as bullying and isolation at school. Whilst reflecting on these experiences with their peers can help children learn new ways of addressing the challenges they face, reflecting on experiences of bullying and isolation at school can be a vehicle for making sense of the powerlessness and uncertainty children face in relation to illness and the threat of death.

Schools: an underutilized resource

School offers children access to experiences that are less dominated by illness. For children who have been ill and been absent for some time, returning to school is an opportunity to engage with people their own age, re-engage with age-appropriate concerns, and focus on their studies. However, although the structured setting of school and the need to focus on school work can help children forget their worries, because they are usually expected to work in silence, some find themselves flooded with anxieties and fears that are easier to keep at bay when active.

The return to school is often a time when children who have been ill and their parents tend to become more aware of their differences in relation to peers. Exposure to life-and-death issues means that their preoccupations are likely to be out of synch with those of their peers. Having spent far more time with adults than with people their own age, they may need to relearn how to engage in an age-appropriate way. In some cases reduced levels of energy, increased vulnerability and worries about their health also mean that they have to develop alternative, less physically demanding ways of interacting with peers.

Moreover, even though their peers might have been exposed to illness before, this may be the first time they realize someone of their age can become so ill (or one's parent or sibling can become so ill), giving rise to curiosity and/or anxiety about their own health and mortality. Fascination with the unusual, a desire to distance oneself from someone who represents what is feared, and concerns about saying the wrong thing are likely to be amongst the reasons that these children are often teased or isolated. This isolation may be self-induced, as even those who are very young realize when their presence is not welcome.

Feelings of difference tend to be heightened when children's appearance is affected and/or the side effects of the treatment are embarrassing. However, even where the disfigurement or side effect is slight and temporary, internalized perceptions of difference can last well beyond the point where this is physically apparent. Worries about being different seem to be equally powerful when the condition is fairly wide spread, as with HIV/AIDs in many regions of sub-Saharan Africa (Cluver et al., 2008).

Issues of difference are particularly important when the capacity for abstract thought and communication is affected. Children who are absent from school at the start of the year seem to struggle most of all, particularly with subjects like maths. Although the move towards integration has made it more possible for children with special needs to engage with peers, unless this is sensitively handled, peers' fears of engaging with someone who is different may mean school is one of the places where this group of children feel most isolated (Brown, 2004). Although careful assessment is needed to ensure they receive appropriate specialized input, where the condition follows a fluctuating course this is more difficult to establish. Because emotional factors can affect concentration and cognitive functioning, it is often unclear whether areas of deficit relate to the physical or the psychological.

As outlined earlier, the boundaries between the family and school tend to become more permeable at times of illness to ensure that a child with a chronic condition receives the practical and emotional support they need (particularly where they need to take medication under adult supervision) and to keep the school up to date with the child's treatment and signs that might signify a deterioration in health, for example, changes in energy and concentration (Bannon and Ross, 1998). In some cases, a support teacher can be brought in to help the child in class. Where the teacher knows the family well, it may be preferable to ask them to work with the rest of the class for a time to allow the teacher to focus more on that child. However, it may be a relief for teachers to be able to share the responsibility for supporting that child.

Growing recognition of the extent to which people are exposed to illness and death at some stage of their childhood and adolescence has led to calls for schools to develop policy statements and guidelines on how to address these experiences at school. Emphasis is placed on such issues as the need to clarify the academic and emotional requirements of the child; how this can be accommodated at school; greater liaison between schools, families and the hospital; where children are not mobile, access to a tutor, and for inpatients, a hospital-based school; and running trainings for teachers on ways of addressing illness and death with children. Although this work focuses almost exclusively on children who are or have been seriously ill, much of what is said in relation to childhood illness is equally relevant to situations where a sibling, parent or another member of the family is seriously ill or dying. However, as helpful as any such guidelines may be, it is important to set aside times in which teachers are able to reflect more freely on such issues as how to:

- Support the child without compromising one's role as an educator.
- Answer the questions discussions about illness and death evoke.
- Protect the child in question without accentuating differences.
- Assist children without deskilling their parents.
- Help children who are absent remain in contact with their class and keep up with as much school work as possible.
- Help children balance their academic and family commitments.
- Provide children with opportunities to experience choice at school as an antidote to the powerlessness they are likely to face elsewhere in their lives.

Regardless of whether the child, their sibling or parent is ill, many turn to teachers to make sense of what is happening to them, particularly when they feel less able to do so at home. However, it can be difficult for teachers to know how to support the child without appearing to be trying to be a 'better parent' (Clay et al., 2004). This is particularly difficult where they are the same gender or age as an ill parent, as the tendency to identify can evoke feelings and fears that are difficult to manage (Altschuler et al., 1999). Respect for the stresses the family is facing at such times means that teachers often delay alerting parents when there are worries about a child's academic performance or behaviour. Although this might be aimed at protecting parents, it robs them of the chance of developing a better understanding of their children's experience and means that by the time they are alerted, the difficulties may have escalated.

However, regardless of whether we work with children at school, in the hospital or in another setting, because the possibilities of personal resonances are greatest with children, it is important to ensure that our ideas of what children need and want relate to their experience rather than our own.

Summary

- Children tend to be more resilient when they can turn to someone who holds their needs in mind, they are able to experience agency and where the family is supportive, optimistic and communicates openly.
- The symbolic importance of parent–child relationships to both parties means that children's responses to illness tend to be bound up with the ways in which their parents respond.
- Whilst separation anxiety tends to be a major concern for the very young, fitting in with peers and having to assume levels of responsibility that are out of keeping with one's age tend to be more important during adolescence.
- Working with children requires us to move beyond the verbal and engage with their play.
- As children spend a great deal of their time at school, school can be an enormous resource when they are faced with illness or death.

5

PARENTING IN THE FACE OF ILLNESS

Regardless of whether we live together or apart, and whether the relationship is supportive or conflicted, parent–child relationships appear to influence understandings of who we are and relationships with others throughout our lives (de Mol and Buysse, 2008). As discussed previously, the child's experience of coming to know her- or himself relies on the parent's capacity to intuit and respond to that child. This means that parents and children are receptive and vulnerable to the attitudes and feelings of the other. As such, it can be difficult to separate one's own experience from that of one's children (Bowlby, 1953, 1980; Stern, 1985).

Every parent will have been through times when they or one of their children are ill, when other aspects of life have to be put on hold to care for a child who is too unwell to attend school, or attend medical appointments. In most cases, the experience is brief and we are able to return to our former lives relatively unaffected. However, this tends to be less feasible when a parent or child has a life-limiting and debilitating condition.

Before discussing the challenges illness presents to parents, it is important to note that although an increased proportion of children live in one-parent or three-generational households, or with parents who are not married and/or are in a same-sex relationship, the majority of the literature on parenting draws on studies of married couples who are in a heterosexual relationship. Although many of the challenges other parents face will be similar, these parents are likely to be faced with challenges that are less known to others.

For example, concerns about exposing children to homophobic teasing means that some parents who are in a same-sex relationship avoid disclosing this aspect of their family life to their child's school. If, however, they feel their children need additional support at times of illness, they may feel forced to be more open with their school. This means that they have to find a way of helping their children make sense of the illness as well as making sense of what this knowledge about their family means to their peers.

Similarly, the few studies of illness that do focus on the experiences of lone parents suggest that their children are more likely to internalize their worries and develop school problems (Kazak, 2006; Pai et al., 2008). However, this need not mean these parents are any less competent than others: instead it may be a reflection of the fact that they are likely to be contending with more financial stress, and reduced access to taken-for-granted support, as well as being more isolated (Brown et al., 2007). Indeed, where the relationship is particularly conflicted, separation and divorce can free parents to focus more of their attention on what their children need.

On parenting an ill child

Finding out that one's child has a life-limiting condition tends to face parents with the need to:

- Educate themselves about the illness and treatment options.
- Collaborate with health care professionals to ensure their child receives the best possible treatment.
- Explain the illness to their children.
- Prepare the ill child for medical procedures, without confronting them and their siblings with information they cannot understand or do not want to know.
- Help their children deal with the feelings of panic that can set in.
- Where the treatment reduces the child's immunity or the condition is contagious, explain what level of contact is safe.
- Model coping behaviour and problem-solving, inspire hope and maintain as much of their children's everyday routines as possible.
- Help children deal with the feelings differences in health status can evoke.
- Schedule in some time with siblings of the ill child to ensure they feel treasured, and offer them the chance to participate in some level of decision making and manageable aspects of care.
- Keep the rest of the family, friends and school informed about significant changes in the illness and treatment while respecting the child's right to privacy.

Coming to terms with loss

Possibly the most painful challenge parents face is relinquishing the dream of bringing up a 'normal' child. When the diagnosis is affirmed at birth, as with many hereditary and birth trauma disorders, feelings of grief can interfere with parents' ability to bond with the child. Weingarten describes the experience of coming to terms with the knowledge that her daughter had a rare genetic disorder as 'falling in love while living in terror' (Weingarten and Wothern, 1997: 47). Where the condition is likely to affect the child's life expectancy, parents are also faced with coming to terms with the loss of an imagined future and possibility of grandchildren. However, because it is not as if anyone has died, these feelings cannot be acknowledged, as reflected in Doka's (1999) concept of 'disenfranchised grief'.

Even if parents have been able to set aside their feelings of sadness and disappointment, key points in the life-cycle can act as reminders of what has been lost, re-evoking a process of grieving. In the case of a first-born child with significant learning disabilities, this might include moments he or she might otherwise have started school, or gone to university, and when younger brothers and sisters are able to reach age-appropriate milestones without any difficulty.

In some cases, finding out that a child is ill and watching them suffer, as, for example, when an asthmatic child cannot breathe, is deeply traumatic. In such situations, parents' capacity to think tends to become paralysed as they muster all their energy into trying to reduce the unmanageable quantities of excitation that pour through this breach in the protective shield we tend to surround ourselves with (Stoppelbein and Greening, 2007). This is particularly likely when parents' own childhood was traumatic. However, even if parents' distress and panic do not reach this level, the experience can trigger feelings that relate to past experiences of loss. As discussed earlier, experiences within our family of origin inform the scripts we draw on in responding to our own children (Byng-Hall, 1985, 1995). These experiences may have left us with the desire to provide our children with the sort of care we were able to receive, or the opposite, to ensure that we treat ours very differently. Despite this, experiences of intense emotion can result in acting in a way that is at odds with these 'corrective' or 'replicative' scripts, giving rise to actions that feel like a betrayal of our children as well as ourselves.

Questions of responsibility and blame

Although all parents will be faced with situations that confront us with how powerless we are, this tends to happen more often when a child is seriously ill or disabled. Some parents are faced with this fairly early on, for example when an infant child cannot feed, is inconsolable, struggles to breathe and needs to be admitted to hospital. Others are faced with experiences of powerlessness at a later stage, as when an adult child becomes seriously ill and parents' own frailty means they cannot offer them (and their children) the sort of support they feel their children need.

Because parents are bigger and stronger than children (when they are young), most parents have the resources to influence their views and experiences. However, because a wide range of other factors including relationships with others play a significant role in children's lives, instead of seeing parents as having 'ultimate responsibility' for children, it is more accurate to think in terms of a 'judicious' or partial responsibility that takes account of the power parents do have as well as other aspects of experience including society's responsibility for ensuring parents are able to care for children (Weingarten, 1994).

Moreover, experiences of responsibility and blame are not confined to the real. Faced with loss and uncertainty we tend to ask ourselves why, why did this happen to me, us, him or her? As discussed before, one of the most common responses to these questions is to blame others, to project what is hated or feared onto someone else or something entirely different, or the opposite, to blame oneself (Benjamin, 1998; Klein, 1975).

Parents of ill children are particularly vulnerable to blaming themselves (or being blamed by others): this is partly because they tend to be seen as their main source of protection and partly because they are often required to play a significant role in their child's treatment. In some cases parents find themselves having to act in ways that contradict their previous beliefs of what good parenting entails, for example by being more watchful of children than feels appropriate for their age or performing procedures that cause pain or discomfort, as in applying forceful physiotherapy to a child with cystic fibrosis.

Although guilt can increase our sensitivity to others, it can also lead to distancing ourselves from the person who embodies these feelings of guilt, in this case one's child, or compensating by holding back on providing any realistic limit setting. The potential to blame oneself or others tends to be greater when the condition is poorly understood, when a deterioration in health could relate to non-adherence or not having taken one's child's symptoms seriously enough, when there is a possibility that the condition may have been caused by a life-style choice, experiences of assault, or is hereditary.

With this in mind, as painful as this might be, it can be helpful to explore parents' beliefs about why their child is ill or was born disabled, and where relevant, encourage them to discuss misunderstandings with a medical member of the team. Where blame seems to be a central feature of their relationship with their children, although it is important to avoid discrediting how they see their experience, it can also be helpful to draw attention to discrepancies in factual information, explore the impact these feelings of blame are having on relationships, and reflect on the emptiness of blame and its failure to avert the course of the condition.

Monitoring and vigilance

As mentioned above, parents are often required to keep a close watch if their child has a chronic condition to make sure they follow the prescribed treatment regime. In some cases, the need for vigilance extends to other areas of their lives, for example to trying to ensure that children avoid overextending themselves when playing with their peers. This can result in heightening parents' sense of responsibility so that even when the child is well, they remain preoccupied with the possibility of a recurrence.

Finding the right balance between being protective and allowing children to engage in age-appropriate activities is extremely difficult. Although engaging with peers and age-appropriate activities can go a long way towards bolstering resilience in the face of difficult circumstances, fear of losing one's child and/or guilt can limit parents' ability to allow children to engage in these activities. Acting in too restrictive a way can mean that children become overly anxious about their health or so frustrated that they rebel against their treatment. However, allowing children too much responsibility means that they are less protected. It also means that if their health deteriorates they are seen to be responsible for this. Adding to the complexity is that parents are rarely given any guidance on what normal living means in these situations (Eiser, 1997).

Moreover, even though there are medical reasons for monitoring one's child's health so closely, this process offers parents some sense of control in a situation that tends to feel uncontrollable. However, the unpredictable nature of many conditions means that establishing some sense of control is rarely feasible. In addition, it can be difficult to know whether changes in the child's level of energy and concentration are signs of deterioration in health that could have been averted, or of how the child feels at an emotional level. This means that any such deterioration can be experienced as a failure.

Mothers tend to be more vigilant about their children's health than is true of fathers. This is likely to relate to the fact that, despite cultural variations and shifts over time, women's sense of self is more likely to be bound up with caring for children than is the case for men. Indeed, 'good' mothers tend to be seen as powerful enough to produce 'healthy' children and bad mothers to produce children who are unhealthy (Weingarten, 1994). However, this does not fit for all families as ideas about gendered roles and expectations are far more fluid than had been assumed.

Nonetheless, certain patterns appear to be common. For example, Sallfors and Hallberg (2003) found that mothers of children with juvenile arthritis see themselves as carrying primary responsibility for that child and are more in touch with the child's emotional and practical needs than is true of fathers. In contrast, fathers have been found to adopt a more marginal role, focusing more of their energy on caring for the rest of the family and ensuring the family is financially viable. This more marginal position may account for why they tend to be more optimistic about their child's health.

It may also account for why fathers are often described as invisible or 'hard to reach' (McConkey, 1994). This need not reflect their actual unavailability but may reflect an underplaying of the roles they do and can play. For example, where the parents of children with significant learning difficulties have separated, fathers are less likely to be included in discussions about their child's progress than mothers, and groups for parents tend to be geared more towards mothers.

With this in mind, it is important to ensure that the care that is on offer is more welcoming and respectful of the role of fathers. For example, where fathers are in full-time employment, this could mean considering whether it is feasible to arrange feedback sessions at times when they are more able to attend, where possible offering parents longer notice about forthcoming medical appointments and offering fathers an opportunity to reflect on the challenges they face, with others who are in a similar position. It could also be helpful to encourage mothers to reflect on the challenges fathers face and the roles they are playing and could play.

Mothering, fathering and couple relationships

The findings of research aimed at understanding the impact of caring for a child with a wide range of medical conditions on couple relationships suggest that parenting a seriously ill child tends to have a negative effect on marital satisfaction and sexual relationships. However, others have found either no difference or that the experience leads to an increased sense of trust, and capacity to communicate and solve problems, and that the rates of divorce are no higher than the norm (Gerhardt et al., 2003; Lavee and May-Dan, 2003).

Nevertheless, experiences such as having to accompany one's child to medical appointments and care for them when they are too ill to attend school tend to interfere with the possibilities of working and maintaining one's usual social activities, facing couples with greater financial difficulties and loss of the self-esteem and companionship that work and interactions with friends can provide (Winthrop et al., 2005). As a result, couples may turn to one another for support far more than before. This is particularly likely when the condition is unusual, as others will have little understanding of the challenges they are facing (Weingarten and Worthen, 1997). Although relying on one another in this way can create a deeper sense of intimacy, this tends to be more difficult when the relationship was hostile before and when one or both parents' earlier experiences of intimacy have been abusive. However, even when these relationships have been more supportive, being faced with one another's grief can feel intolerable.

In some cases, this is the first time parents are confronted with the way in which their partner responds to situations of loss and powerlessness, revealing differences they were unaware of before. For example, they may find that although one parent needs to talk about their distress, their partner finds physical comfort more important than words or finds it easier to cope by denying the seriousness of their child's condition. They may also find that they have different ideas about whether it is appropriate to confront medical professionals when they have doubts about their child's care. Moreover, all parents have somewhat different views about certain aspects of parenting and over time reach an unstated agreement about how to deal with their differences. This may involve each person taking responsibility for particular aspects of parenting, trying to meet one another half way, one parent silencing their own views in the interests of presenting a unified front, or arguing each time these differences feel important.

A certain level of difference can be extremely helpful: indeed, one parent's sense of optimism can go a long way towards balancing the pessimism of the other. Moreover, holding on to differences and arguing with one another can be a way of breathing life into one's relationship at a time when couples feel ground down by feelings of grief and powerlessness. Nonetheless, adopting polarized positions tends to limit partners' ability to recognize what is shared and reach decisions about their ill child and other aspects of family life. Some differences are based on misunderstandings and exposure to different sorts of information. However, as discussed earlier, our views on what good parenting entails tend to be informed by our own experience of being parented. Although this is not always possible, reflecting on the links with past experiences can help parents develop a wider understanding of their differences, increasing their readiness to find a compromise that is comfortable to both parties.

Gender offers another useful frame for widening understandings of difference. For example, research suggests that mothers and fathers tend to react differently to the news that a child is seriously ill, that mothers (and where mothers are unavailable, female members of the family and community) carry a greater level of responsibility for caring for that child, and that women are more able to have access to wider social networks of support than is true of men (Herbert and Carpenter, 2007). Research also suggests that even if women hold positions of considerable authority at work, they often acquiesce to men at home. However, parenting an ill child tends to disrupt this balance of power.

For example, as mothers are more likely to assume primary responsibility for caring for the ill child, they are likely to have greater contact with the medical team than their partner and as such need to become the family expert on the child's condition. Although this means that mothers are more vulnerable to self-blame and the criticism of others, where they had assumed a more subservient position in relation to their partner before, the experience can increase their sense of agency and self-esteem. Moreover, although most societies place a lower value on caring for children than the world of paid employment, fathers who had spent relatively little time caring for their children on their own before may find that engaging with them on a more ongoing basis alters their understanding of their children, themselves and the roles their partners have played.

Although it is rarely easy to talk about or accept significant changes in the balance of power in a relationship that is deeply important to us, raising these personal frustrations is likely to feel trivial or even selfish when a child is seriously ill. It is likely to be even more difficult when the relationship is hostile and conflicted and when illness is used to make claims that relate to other aspects of the relationship. In these circumstances, parents might need the space to address their relational differences before being able to focus on the needs of their children.

Relationships with extended family and friends

As discussed previously, although most families construct a fairly impermeable boundary between themselves and the outside world, this tends to become more permeable when a child is ill to ensure that they and others receive the care they need. For example, the need to spend time with an ill child in hospital or take them to appointments means that they may have to ask members of the extended family or friends to take their children to school and after-school activities.

Members of the extended family can be enormously helpful when a child is seriously ill. If the relationship has been mutually supportive, relying on one's family can be relatively uncomplicated. However, it tends to be more difficult when these relationships are and have always been hostile. In some cases, parents find out that the rest of the family are more willing to help than they had imagined. Nonetheless, this is not always the case: where relationships are extremely fraught, even if family members have been supportive at times of crisis, this need not affect other aspects of their relationship. Moreover, where families have migrated or live in different parts of the country, they are rarely able to offer the hands-on support that is needed other than at moments of particular crisis.

As with members of the extended family, friends are often willing to help at times of crisis as well, particularly if this does not involve considerable inconvenience. However, they are often unsure of what is needed and are likely to benefit from being told or asked what to do. Moreover, few are willing to do this on a longer-term basis. Indeed, many are wary of taking on the additional responsibility this is likely to entail (Dale, 1997). As a result, parents of seriously ill children tend to feel extremely isolated (Famuyiwa and Akinyanju, 1998). In some ways, this isolation is partly self-inflicted: although being with friends offers parents access to conversations about other aspects of life, worries about burdening one's friends, and friends' own worries about discussing issues that seem trivial by comparison, can mean that instead of being invigorating, being together is a strain. Being together can also be a strain when it means having to keep up with others' need to know more. Whilst the questions they ask may relate to a genuine desire to be supportive, they are also likely to be informed by a need to know what to say to their own children and a desire for reassurance about their own children's health. With this in mind, it can be extremely helpful if one friend or member of the extended family is willing to act as a conduit for sharing information with the rest of one's friends and family.

On being an ill parent

With the exception of palliative care and HIV/AIDs services, parents who are diagnosed with a life-limiting condition are rarely offered help in thinking about the impact their being ill might have on their children and their experience of parenting. For example, in their study of women with breast cancer, Barnes et al. (2000) found that mothers were rarely asked about their children and how they would tell them about the diagnosis, or offered guidance on the impact their diagnosis might have for their children.

The reasons for this omission are likely to include that medical professionals tend to have fairly limited time with adult patients, that one professional does not hold an overall responsibility for their psychological and physical wellbeing, fears about being unable to answer the questions parents raise and/or fears that talking about their children might increase parents' distress and have a negative effect on their physical wellbeing. Parents are often reticent about discussing their children with the medical team as well. This is likely to reflect similar concerns about safeguarding the time they have to discuss their medical condition and fears that instead of helping, talking about their children could compound the difficulties they are already facing.

In view of the value health care professionals attach to psycho-social support, this omission suggests that engaging more fully with the consequences parental illness can have for children is too threatening, possibly because it challenges the idealized notion that parents are able to protect their children from harm. Instead of being helpful, failing to engage with this does not help in reducing parents' concerns or mean that children will not be affected: instead it means that parents tend to be faced with making sense of the disruptions this poses to their anticipated experiences of parenting on their own. However, this is starting to shift, as reflected in an EU-wide study aimed at identifying what limits the likelihood of children of somatically ill parents developing long-term psychological difficulties (Gericke, 2002). Many of the challenges parents face when they or their partner is seriously ill are similar to those outlined in discussing childhood illness. For example, here too, parents have to find a way of familiarizing themselves with the medical condition, explaining to their children what this entails, helping them make sense of what this means for their own lives, coming to terms with loss and, where parents are in an ongoing couple relationship, developing a shared understanding of what good parenting means in these circumstances. However, what is different is that when parents are ill there are likely to be times when they have to prioritize their own needs for care over that of their children; when they are less able to offer the sort of care they had imagined giving their children and are faced with the fact that events in their own life could have a damaging effect on their children.

Balancing self-care with caring for others

One of the most difficult challenges parents face is that although prioritizing the needs of one's children is seen as integral to being a good parent in most societies, this is less feasible when one has a life-limiting illness or is severely disabled. Questions about whether or not to prioritize one's own care often relate to everyday events, for example on whether to preserve one's energies or collect one's children from school, take them to after-school activities and cook the family meal. These questions may also relate to whether or not to put one's children to bed earlier than usual when one is too exhausted and upset to cope, and at risk of saying or doing something that is regretted later.

One way of helping parents to address these feelings is by framing prioritizing their own needs as a way of caring for their children: because prioritizing one's own health maximizes the chances of healing; the likelihood of children having to contend with a parent who is more unwell than necessary or dies is reduced. However, to do this requires a significant shift in the expectations they and others have of their role.

Because women's sense of identity tends to be more bound up with caring for children and other vulnerable family members than is true of men, prioritizing their own care tends to be more difficult for mothers than fathers (Weingarten, 1994). Men who become seriously ill seem to find it easier to accept their need for care but tend to find it more difficult to relinquish instrument tasks. Nonetheless, as discussed in relation to childhood illness, where fathers played a less central role in caring for children before, spending more time at home to recuperate from treatment can result in developing a different connection with their children and placing a higher priority on family relationships. However, it can be difficult to acknowledge these gains as they have resulted from the diagnosis of a life-limiting illness.

It can also be difficult for the healthy partner to know how much to take on without undermining the other parent. Encouraging ill parents to share their understanding of the children's needs and 'tutor' their partner helps to ensure their children receive the care that they need. If parents are dying, sharing these thoughts with their partner can go a long way towards ensuring that their children will be cared for as they had hoped, when they are no longer there. However, this is less feasible when the condition affects the person's mental functioning and personality. For example, Adam had been diagnosed with leukodystrophy, a progressive degenerating condition that had resulted in his becoming increasingly disinhibited and acting in an aggressive way. As a result, although he wanted to be more engaged with his children, his partner could not trust him to be alone with them.

Questions of blame and guilt

The assumption that parents should be able to protect children from exposure to harm means it is not unusual to feel guilty about the effect being ill has on one's children. The potential to see oneself as harmful is more likely when the condition has a genetic component or the disease has been transmitted to a child: although Busiswe had been able to come to terms with her own diagnosis of HIV/AIDs, it was far more difficult to come to terms with the knowledge that the virus had been transmitted to her son.

Feelings of guilt may relate to times when parents are less available to their children. For example, hospital admissions and medical appointments can interfere with parents' ability to take their children to school and after-school activities or participate in family meals and bedtime rituals. There may be times when pain, weariness and nausea mean that parents' primary pre-occupation is with their body rather than with those with whom they are most intimately connected. Indeed, even if parents live together, the anxiety, fear and guilt parents feel may mean that there are times when both parents are 'emotionally absent' despite being physically present (Boss, 2006).

One of the consequences of guilt is that it can limit parents' ability to discipline their children. This is particularly likely when children are required to care for their parent in ways that are well beyond their years, as is often the case with adolescent daughters. Rivas's (2003) analysis of interactions between disabled adults and paid carers suggests that many disabled adults fail to cast a 'reciprocal gaze' on the experience of carers, in what seems to be an attempt to preserve an image of the self as independent. Although there are important differences between the positions of paid and family carers, this study offers some insight into why parents, and to some extent professionals, tend to avoid focusing their 'gaze' on the consequences that caring for an ill and disabled parent have for the child and their relationship with their family.

Supporting parents facing illness

The stresses and strains caused by experiences of childhood and parental illness mean most parents will benefit from an opportunity to meet with a member of the medical team to reflect on the consequences illness has for themselves and their children, regardless of whether they appear to be having particular difficulties or not.

As it is often difficult to remember what is said in an emotionally loaded context, it is useful to offer parents a written leaflet which summarizes the more common ways in which children respond, ways of talking with children about illness, and experiences that can help children hold on to a sense of security despite the presence of serious illness. One of the other advantages of a leaflet is that it makes it more possible to share what has been said with other people who play a central role in the child's life. Needless to say, when working with parents who are not fluent in English, these leaflets need to be translated into other languages.

As reflected in the proliferation of self-help websites and organizations for parents, many parents find it helpful to connect with others who are in a similar position. In hospital settings, this tends to happen on an informal basis, for example while waiting for a medical appointment. However, as there is rarely enough time or privacy to address more problematic concerns, it can be helpful to offer parents a chance to meet in a more structured group setting, be this on a one-off or a more ongoing basis. As discussed in relation to children, in each case the aim is to create a context in which parents feel able to discuss illness-related dilemmas with people who have an insider experience of the challenges they face, learn from one another and disentangle concerns that relate to their unusual situation from concerns that are particular to their own family. Although it is important to leave time for fairly open discussion, group sessions tend to be more effective when they include psycho-educational input and are led by a professional who has an understanding of group dynamics and experience of working with families facing illness (Broome and Stuart, 2005; Campbell, 2003).

A number of parents tend to need more intensive psychological support. In some cases, parents and their families are referred because someone else, be this a teacher or doctor, feels they or their children are struggling. In other cases, they ask for additional support themselves. This need not mean that they or their children are more troubled than others: it may mean that they place a high priority on parenting and the wellbeing of their children.

For example, although Angie was seen by a hospital psychologist following the diagnosis of a particularly aggressive form of cancer, she asked to be seen by someone who worked outside of the hospital to reflect on the impact her diagnosis was having on herself and her children, Ollie aged eleven and Nathalie aged eight.

In an initial meeting with Angie, I learned that she had told her children about her diagnosis and that the treatment she was receiving would make her better, but avoided using the word 'cancer' for fear that conversations with others would lead to the belief she would die. I also learned that the relationship between her and her children's father Jude had been difficult for a long time and they were on the brink of separating when she was diagnosed. Her diagnosis strengthened her resolve to separate as she saw her diagnosis as a sign that their relationship was not only damaging at an emotional level but had been damaging to her health. At her insistence her ex-partner Jude agreed to leave the family home. However, although he agreed that their relationship was problematic, he felt separating would compound the difficulties Ollie and Nathalie would have in coming to terms with their mother's diagnosis.

The work included sessions with Angie and Jude on their own, and sessions with one or both parents and their children. Although Jude continued to play a significant role in caring for their children, Angie relied on her mother more than previously. Because their relationship had always been fraught, they were seen together on several occasions as well.

Where parents like Angie seem unable or unwilling to understand what their children are going through, it can be helpful to work towards increasing their curiosity about their children's experience, for example by asking them to imagine or role-play how they might feel or respond if they were in their children's position and encouraging them to reflect on their own experiences of, in this case, being eleven and eight. Exercises like these enabled Angie to recognize that her children knew more and were far more worried than she had wanted to acknowledge. This led to the decision to invite them to a session with her and later with both parents. At these sessions their questions and drawings suggested that they were afraid their mother would die and extremely distressed about their parents' decision to separate. As such, although these sessions became a forum for talking about their mother's illness and the impact it was having and might have on their lives, it was also a forum for making sense of their parents' decision to separate. As Nathalie, the younger of the two, asked if her parents 'couldn't at least try' to stay together, their parents used these sessions to explain that this was their decision and that even though they might not love one another any more this did not mean they loved their children less. Because children often blame themselves when a parent is ill or parents separate, this included helping them understand that neither situation was their fault.

At times, anger about the ways in which they had been treated by each other in the past meant that Angie and Jude were less able to focus on the children. However, although there were times when they returned to these past difficulties, as with all post-separation work, to avoid discussions about the past becoming a replaying of old arguments, it was important to try to focus on what their children needed at this point in the present. This included asking questions about times when they had been able to work together, in order to help them reconnect with their sense of competence as parents, and establish a less incriminating view of themselves and each other. It also included trying to separate difficulties that were an almost inevitable consequence of situations of parental illness, from other relational difficulties.

When I saw the family last, Angie was clear of the cancer. However, where the condition is terminal, members of the family often differ in how much they want to acknowledge to themselves, each other and their children that the person is dying. One of the difficulties is that failing to acknowledge the end is near can isolate members of the family from one another, creating tension and regrets that complicate subsequent experiences of mourning. Consequently, even if the dying person is no longer able to speak, it is important to encourage people to reach out to one another, as a touch, a smile or moment of eye contact can be enormously sustaining for those who are dying as well as the survivors. As devastating as it may be to know one will not be able to be there as one's children become adults and parents themselves, parents can find it helpful to think about ways of enabling their children to hold on to the memory of who they were and their relationship with them.

Summary

- Regardless of whether they or their child has a life-limiting condition, experiences of illness face parents with the challenges of:

o Coming to terms with loss
o Balancing the demands of the illness with other aspects of family life
o Helping children make sense of their experience and preparing them for the reactions of others
o Separating their own experience from that of their children
o Maintaining intergenerational boundaries and discipline
o Resolving differences in approach to parenting.

- Challenges that are more particular to childhood illness include monitoring the child's health, balancing the need to protect with encouraging children to engage in age-related activities, and helping the ill and healthy children make sense of their differences.
- Challenges that are more particular to parental illness include having to balance one's own needs for care with caring for others, and dealing with the feelings of guilt this tends to evoke.
- All parents are likely to benefit from an opportunity to reflect on the dilemmas illness presents to their roles as parents, written guidance on the impact illness can have on children, and the possibility of meeting parents in a similar position.
- However, parents who are struggling are likely to benefit from more intensive individual, couple or family work.

6

ILLNESS AND ADULT RELATIONSHIPS

The diagnosis of a life-limiting condition tends to create a disjunction between anticipated and lived experiences, impacting on adults' relationship with and belief in the predictability of the body, taken-for-granted relationships, finances and prospects of future employment (Bury, 1982).

Where the condition is chronic, adults have to find a way of constructing a sense of normalcy in a context in which being healthy is seen as the norm, and where their own sense may be of hovering between enduring and trying to escape the suffering they face (Ohman et al., 2003). In contrast, when the condition is terminal, the thoughts and concerns of the dying person and their loved ones are more likely to focus on the future, on how much longer they have together, whether there will be time to put their affairs in order, and in the case of conditions like cancer, whether it will be possible to manage the pain, without having to rely too much on medication that affects their emotional and cognitive functioning. There are also likely to be concerns about future finances and how the survivors will cope when they are not able to offer the support and guidance their loved ones need.

Research and clinical experience suggests that adults are more able to offset the stresses and challenges these experiences present if there is access to an intimate and confiding relationship in which it is possible to feel listened to and understood (Helgeson and Novak, 2006). Factors like gender, class, culture, ethnicity and prior experiences of loss appear to have a significant impact on responses to illness, affecting the frequency with which symptoms are reported, perceptions of severity, levels of anxiety and the 'real' and perceived quality of care (Kristofferzon et al., 2003). While some people find solace in their religious and spiritual beliefs, others find this meaning-less (Koenig et al., 2001). In addition, while some tend to adopt a 'problem-focused style of coping', as in focusing most of their energy on trying to do something about the actual illness and treatment, others adopt more of an 'emotion-focused' style, as in trying to lessen distress by avoidance, selective attention and denial (Folkman, 1997). Moreover, these patterns are not necessarily fixed as styles of coping that prove helpful at one point may have little bearing on what is help-ful at the next.

The responses of people who have recovered from a life-threatening condition vary as well: for example, while some cancer survivors seem able to return to their former life relatively unaffected, others find that their lives remain dominated by anxiety and depression or that their earlier priorities are unrealistic or no longer desirable (Anderson and Geist Martin, 2003; Little et al., 2002).

Age and changes in the family life course

The changes adults undergo as we become older are less obvious than is true of children and adolescents. Nonetheless, age and positions in the life cycle of the family can have a profound effect on adult expe-riences of illness. For example, as discussed earlier, when an adult becomes seriously ill for longer or briefer periods of time, the energies of the whole family tend to focus inwards to maximize their chances of healing and survival. This tends to shift once the crisis has abated, enabling the family to redirect their energies towards other aspects of experience, towards events and relationships in the outside world. As there tends to be a similar shift in focus as families move across the life course, the challenges the ill person and the rest of their family face vary depending on whether illness strikes at a stage when the person in question operates on an independent basis or their energy focuses more on the family, as when there are young children (Rolland, 1994).

Because a significant proportion of the population establish a rela-tionship with someone who becomes their life partner when in their twenties and thirties, the diagnosis of a life-limiting condition and the diagnosis of illness at this time (or death of a parent) can set the tone for future patterns of dependency and care. Where the condition is extremely incapacitating, and the treatment requirements are exten-sive, people who are single may not have the energy to establish new relationships, study or work. Even if they have left home, the need for additional support may force them to rely more on their parents or siblings and/or move in with them.

Where there is a possibility of becoming progressively more disabled, as with multiple sclerosis or motor neurone disease, concerns about becoming a burden to others and the risks of pregnancy can result in a decision to stay single. Where people are in a couple relationship, and pregnancy is not possible or too dangerous to the potential mother or the child, artificial insemination, surrogacy and adoption are options that can be considered. However, taking this step may require a reworking of one's beliefs about what 'authentic' mothering and fathering entails (Yngvesson and Mahoney, 2000). Guilt, disappointment and the desire to protect one another can mean that one or both partners hold back on expressing their own view. Although this might be aimed at minimizing the differences in their positions, it tends to gives the message that one's partner is too fragile to hear one's views and, as such, is more likely to accentuate rather than minimize these differences.

As adults establish more permanent relations and become parents, most partners reach an unstated understanding of the sort of support they want and are prepared to give each other. This usually needs to be extended to maximize the chances of survival and adjust to the relational skews that tend to develop when one partner is healthy and the other seriously ill. Even if no one is ill, becoming a parent tends to have an enormous impact on relationships, altering partners' availability to one another, experiences of intimacy and need for privacy. Whilst becoming a parent can increase couples' understanding of one another, leading to a greater sense of intimacy, it can face parents with differences they were unaware of before. In some cases, the threat of loosing one another can help partners see these differences in a different light. However, this is not always the case. Where differences in views about parenting become blurred with differences in health status, it is important to offer partners help in separating these two layers of experience.

When illness strikes in later life, as discussed in the next chapter, people are more likely to be contending with other concerns about their health and other forms of loss such as retirement and the death of friends and family of their own age. Moreover, many older adults do not have a partner, and if they do, their partners are often frail or ill themselves. As such, when a life-long partner requires supervised residential care, the healthier partner has to decide whether or not to move with them, facing them with the loss of their home, life style and independence at the same time as coming to terms with the knowledge of how unwell their partner is (Kriseman and Claes, 1997).

Disruptions to patterns of intimacy

It has long been recognized that intimate, confiding relationships provide a buffer against becoming depressed when faced with ongoing stress and situations that lie beyond one's immediate control (Berg and Upchurch, 2007). As discussed in Chapter 2, infants' early experiences of attachment and separation in relation to their primary care taker appear to influence subsequent experiences of relationships, perceptions of support and the tendency to seek support from others (Collins and Feeney, 2004).

Although there are obviously enormous differences between the experiences of adults and infants, there seems to be some parallel between these earlier experiences of attachment and adults' attachment to a partner. For example, where partners respond consistently and positively to one another's requests for closeness, people are able to experience secure attachment relationships. However, this is not the case when partners are inconsistent and veer between reacting positively and rejecting requests for support (Asendorpf and Wilpers, 2000). As such, it is hardly surprising that there appears to be a strong link between high levels of criticism, defensiveness, marital dissatisfaction and divorce, and between marital conflict and physiological functioning in relation to a wide range of conditions including heart failure and diabetes. This link seems to be evident regardless of whether couples are young newly weds or have been together far longer (Keicolt-Glaser and Newton, 2001; Manne, 1998).

Factors like class inform experiences and expectations of intimacy. For example, middle-class cultures tend to prioritize the sharing of innermost thoughts and feelings, whereby one person discloses something important about themselves and the other responds in a way that makes them feel validated, understood and cared for, while working-class cultures place greater emphasis on providing financial security, protection and meeting one's responsibilities. However, the sharing of thoughts and feelings tends to be more reflective of the assumptions middle-class women hold than is the case for men (Rolland, 1994).

Cultural factors inform experiences and expectations of intimacy as well: while western cultures tend to frame relational intimacy in terms of couple relationships, eastern and African cultures tend to attach greater importance to experiences of intimacy with other people who are part of the individuals' family and social network (Krause, 1998). Similarly, western cultures tend to prioritize the ability to maintain some sense of autonomy, to hold on to a sense of who one is as an individual, as integral to experiences of intimacy, many other cultures prioritize a greater level of interdependency (Bowen, 1978; Collins and Feeney, 2004). However, it is important to avoid operating on the basis of cultural stereotypes: even in western societies, the desire (and tolerance) for greater interdependency varies and people's most intimate and confiding relationships are not necessarily with a partner but may be with a friend or another member of their family.

Nonetheless, in most cases couple intimacy tends to function within a comfort zone that increases or decreases during the course of the relationship, with partners reaching an unstated agreement on how much to disclose to one another. However, this may need to change when one of them is seriously ill, to allow each person the space they need to make sense of their own experience as well as develop a shared understanding of what they want and need from each other, decide what changes are needed, and confront the possibility of death. Moreover, although we might have imagined we would be able to turn to one another at times of particular difficulty, this may feel impossible as moments of closeness tend to increase our awareness of what we might (or are about to) lose.

Research and clinical experience suggest that couples are more able to offset the burdens of illness, disability and the threat of death when they are able to embrace rather than steer clear of the emotional and practical challenges these experiences present. However, couple relationships are not always supportive or mutually satisfying: just because one partner is seriously ill, this does not mean the more ordinary differences and difficulties disappear. Indeed, the illness may have struck at a time when partners were particularly angry or disappointed in one another. In some cases, illness becomes a catalyst for introducing changes that are more sustaining to both partners. This is more likely when partners are responsive to one another, and able to tolerate difference and being dependent on one another. However, this is not always the case: indeed, finding out one has a life-limiting condition can lead to the decision to separate.

Where illness (or an accident) results in cognitive impairment but people are able to remember certain things, talking about the past, looking at photographs and reading poems and music they have enjoyed together can help them and their loved one to hold on to some of what they have shared. Although these moments may only be temporary they can be enormously sustaining. Nonetheless, they also tend to be painful reminders of what has been lost.

It is obviously more difficult to maintain a sense of intimacy when there is a more significant level of cognitive impairment, when the capacity to communicate is significantly reduced and there are marked changes in personality. Since social support is central to bolstering resilience in such situations, it is important to encourage the partner who is well to look to others for support.

Sexual intimacy

For many couples, sexual intimacy is integral to their experience of emotional closeness. However, as reflected in situations of abuse, the act of sex may have little to do with emotional connection. Nevertheless, in a life that is restricted by illness, a satisfactory sexual relationship can be a powerful source of comfort and pleasure, a chance to feel 'normal' and an affirmation of gender when many other aspects of identity have been stripped away (Hodern and Currow, 2003; McInnes, 2003).

However, illness, particularly chronic conditions, can mean that it is more difficult to maintain a sexual relationship that is sustaining to both partners. For example, experiences of fatigue, nausea, pain, and reduced cardiovascular functioning, physical sensation and mobility are likely to limit the range of sexual activity that is possible. In some cases, worries about pushing one's partner too far, irrational fears of contamination and feelings of disgust become so pronounced that one or both parties find it difficult to consider any sexual contact. In addition, the feelings of fear, anxiety, embarrassment and reduced self-esteem that experiences of grief and the threat of death tend to evoke can affect the capacity to become aroused. Moreover, even if one is able to feel aroused, resentment about the relational skews that tend to develop can sour the experience.

Surgical procedures and the side effects of the medication can alter the way people look, impacting on their sense of body image. For example, because a woman's breasts tend to be seen as symbols of femininity, attractiveness and sexuality, procedures that affect the breast tend to challenge women's confidence and enjoyment of their body. Moreover, the physical discomfort that follows a mastectomy or lumpectomy and realization that a part of the body that was associated with sexual pleasure and breast-feeding was cancerous can mean that they do not want their breast to be touched for some time (White, 2000).

Some people struggle more than others when their sex lives are affected. Where sexual intimacy has been fraught, being ill offers couples a respite from their disappointment in one another, freeing them to enjoy less highly charged physical contact and pleasuring such as stroking and cuddling. In other cases, the emotional intensity that surrounds the experiences of illness can lead to an increased sense of arousal. Although this may not be true of both partners, dependence on an able-bodied partner and the fear of hurting an ill partner's feelings may mean that it is difficult to refuse their sexual advances.

Because the relationship is a reminder of illness, some ill and healthy partners turn to another person for sexual comfort and closeness. Even if they have an open understanding about extra-marital relationships, experiences of disclosure can be extremely painful. Where the condition can be sexually transmitted, there is a need to reach some agreement on how one's sex life needs to change, but the shame that tends to be associated with sexually transmitted diseases means that this can be difficult to achieve. For example, as one of the main ways of contracting the HIV virus is through sexual contact, pregnancy may be the first time one or both partners learn they are HIV positive, and that one of them finds out that there have been other sexual partners. Consequently, it can be extremely difficult to separate these two layers of experiences.

Where the person has infected someone they are close to, the risk of suicide tends to increase (Walker, 1991). For example, Pat only found out that her partner was HIV positive and was afraid he had infected her after he committed suicide. As such, her mourning was complicated by the fact that there had been other sexual partners and that although she had believed they had a close relationship she had not realized how troubled he was.

Nonetheless, with important exceptions, people are rarely offered any help in addressing the sexual concerns that can arise. One explanation may be that medical trainings place greater emphasis on addressing physical health than the emotional and sexual concerns people might have. However, this omission is likely to reflect a wider social discomfort with the idea that people who are ill and disabled might still want or have sex. Patients and/or their partners seem to be equally reluctant to raise sexual concerns with their doctor, and are often embarrassed about wanting sex when they are sick, old or both, or unaware that their sexual difficulties relate to their medical condition or treatment.

Because many people are unused to talking about their sex lives and acknowledging sexual needs to a partner in verbal terms, it can be difficult to ask what they can expect from one another or explore other forms of sexual expression, physical intimacy and companionship. As such, it is important to offer people a chance to reflect on the implications for their sex lives with someone who is able to offer practical advice as well as emotional support as a matter of course, rather than waiting for problems to arise.

Health status, power and dependency

One of the most difficult challenges couples face is coming to terms with the shifts in power and dependency that are almost inevitable when one person becomes more of a carer and the other the cared for. The almost 'moral' value most societies place on being healthy means that accommodating to these shifts is likely to be difficult for most people. However, it tends to be particularly difficult where the ill person and/or their partner places a high value on independence, personal control and physical strength, where the relationship was based on treating one another as equals and where the person in need of care had been seen as strong and the other as weak. It also tends to be particularly difficult when people feel (or are made to feel) that they are to blame and when the relationship was unsupportive before, as the differences in health status and caring roles can be used to make claims that relate to other aspects of their relationship.

Research and clinical experience suggests that care giving need not affect the overall satisfaction of the relationship between couples and, in some cases, becomes a catalyst that allows them to develop a more positive sense of self and relationship with one another. People who are ill and disabled appear to cope better when their carers are able to help them to retain as much dignity and independence as possible. However, care giving is never one way: even if people are severely ill and disabled, the quality of support they are able to give their partners (or other carers) can go a long way in helping them cope with the demands they face. Therefore it is interesting to note that, as mentioned previously, Rivas's (2003) analysis of the interaction between disabled adults and paid carers suggests that one of the ways disabled people are able to retain an image of themselves as independent is by failing to cast a 'reciprocal gaze' on the person on whom they are dependent (Rivas, 2003). This suggests that failing to acknowledge the challenges one's partner (or another family carer) is facing may be a way of avoiding facing the reality of how dependent one has become.

Even where the relationship is supportive, care giving can stretch partners beyond the limits of what feels tolerable. Factors like embarrassment or guilt about one's own health status can result in the fact of being a carer subsuming all other aspects of one's life, so that people neglect their own personal needs. Nonetheless, until recently, relatively little attention was paid to the challenges carers face in coming to terms with the changes in the person with whom they are intimately connected and in the expectations they and others have of their roles.

This seems to be shifting. A growing body of research suggests that the quality of support carers are required to provide plays a more important role in determining how stressful the experience of care giving is than the amount of support that is required: for example, providing emotional support and attending to personal tasks like dressing and feeding appear to be more stressful than non-personal tasks like shopping and driving. There are also suggestions that carers can become more dependent on, and experience higher levels of stress than, the person they are caring for (Brennan and Moynihan, 2004; Cousins et al., 2002).

With this in mind, it is important to prepare people fairly early on for the challenges care giving can present, for example during a medical consultation or a one-off session with a counsellor. Normalizing the anger, sadness, fear and guilt that can arise and sharing the fact that some people find themselves saying things that are regretted later go a long way towards 'detoxifying' the experience and counterbalancing the secrecy and guilt that tends to surround these experiences.

However, it is important to pace what is said with the positions of each person in mind, respect the fears both people may have about being overwhelmed, assess what feels manageable and, where relevant, help people place a limit on 'care giver' and 'cared for' roles. For example, it can be helpful to share that many people find they are more able to offset the burdens of long-term experiences of illness, disability and care giving when it is possible to revise their understanding of relationships so that it embraces rather than steers clear of the challenges these experiences tend to present. It is also likely to be helpful to know that people are more able to cope when it is possible to hold on to aspects of their relationship that are not only about illness, and they are able to see aspects of their experience as shared rather than purely individual (Kayser et al., 2007).

Unlike professionals who are paid to care for people while at work, informal carers (including partners and other family members) are expected, and often expect themselves, to provide emotional and practical support without respite or receiving support in their own right. Moreover, many do not see themselves as carers and feel that their actions are based on a relationship of mutual concern in which there is an unstated obligation to care (Brennan and Moynihan, 2004).

Most caregivers are more ready to speak about the person who is ill or disabled than about themselves. The difficulty of prioritizing the position of the other person is that it limits the possibility of exploring alternative ways of addressing the issues carers find most challenging. It is only by expressing one's own voice as a carer that it becomes possible to think about being relieved from tasks one finds most challenging, or asking others for help with shopping. However, unless there is some acknowledgement of what is shared, emphasizing the differences in their positions tends to exacerbate the relational skews that are an almost inevitable consequence of illness and disability, limiting partners' ability to hold on to aspects of identity that are not just about being a carer and being cared for.

Gendered experiences of care

As discussed earlier, despite considerable shifts in assumptions and expectations, the gendered discourses that dominate the societies in which we live tend to have a profound impact on the ways we experience and respond to illness, including the ways in which we describe and understand symptoms, adjust to incapacity, and express emotions, experiences and expectations of support.

Nonetheless, considerable controversy surrounds the question of gendered differences (Gabriel, 1999). Particularly in the west, women tend to live longer than men and have lower rates of mortality in relation to most causes of death, and are more resistant to infectious and degenerative disease. However, women tend to report physical and mental illness more often than men and are more frequent users of health care services.

One explanation is that it is culturally more acceptable for women to report illness than it is for men and that the sick role is more compatible with women's other role responsibilities. Other possible explanations are that women experience more symptoms because the roles they play are more stressful, that men experience fewer symptoms of distress at times of loss (including illness) than is true of women and that men deal differently with their grief, internally or through external actions, both of which are less measurable than outward expressions of distress (Koopmans and Lamers, 2007; Schofield et al., 2000).

Although being married is linked with better health, and exposure to ongoing strain has less negative consequences when married, the benefits seem to be greater for men. Women who are carers tend to experience higher levels of distress than men in a similar position and assume disproportionate amounts of the responsibility for household chores and organizing the family regardless of whether they or their partner is ill.

While the adjustment of both partners is better when the person who is ill is a man, men tend to find it more difficult than women when the person who is ill is a woman (Ell et al., 1998; Pitceathly and Maguire, 2003). Although several factors might account for this, one explanation is that, as discussed previously, the tasks that have traditionally been associated with men continue to be more highly valued in most societies. When illness forces women to assume responsibility for the tasks of a male partner, the shift in their position is more likely to be experienced as growth-inducing and confirming than is the case when men take more responsibility for the family and home on behalf of their female partner. Gender appears to inform the way in which physical symptoms are experienced and viewed: because men are seen to be at greater risk of developing heart failure, there tends to be an underplaying of the seriousness of symptoms in women amongst providers as well as recipients of health care (Harjai et al., 2000).

Moreover, research and clinical experience suggest that women tend to show their distress more openly, talk about feelings, find comfort in recounting experiences, offer comfort to others and seek support from a partner, extended family, friends and professionals. In contrast, men are more likely to fear being powerless and losing control over their feelings, focus their attention on problem-solving, find refuge in work, withdraw, deal with their feelings in private, become defensive and self-protective if pressed about feelings, and seek comfort from a partner or new sexual partner rather than friends and other family members (Lorber and Moore, 2002).

As such, reflecting on gendered experiences and asking questions that challenge gendered assumptions can open up alternative ways of understanding situations in which one person is seen as right and the other as wrong.

Same-sex relationships

Many of the issues discussed above are equally relevant to people who are in a same-sex relationship. In common with all couples, people who are gay and lesbian are likely to have had little understanding of what it means to live with the losses, uncertainties and relational skews that tend to develop in situations of illness and disability when they decided to commit themselves to this relationship.

However, what is different is that their experiences will be informed by discourses pertaining to same-sex relationships that dominate the society in which they live. For example, in most societies, same-sex relationships do not have the social recognition of marriage, which helps to ensure that parents and other family members acknowledge and support their attachment to one another. This is reflected in gaps in terminology: there is no consensus on whether to call a daughter or son's long-term partner a girlfriend, lover or partner, or how to denote parents' position in relation to a child's same-sex partner. Moreover, outside of particular social circles, there are rarely any prescribed rituals to help and guide couples' functioning at times of distress (Fobair et al., 2001; Green and Mitchell, 2002).

Very little academic attention has been paid to understanding the challenges illness presents to this group of people. However, clinical experience suggests that they are more likely to be exposed to prejudicial treatment by health care professionals than others. In addition, when they have worries about their relationship with one another or their children, the desire to avoid homophobia impacting on their medical care means that they are more likely to seek additional emotional support from an agency that has no connection with their treatment.

The picture is somewhat different for gay men with the HIV virus. Anxiety that HIV/AIDs might increase the level of homophobia in the societies in which they live have had the effect of mobilizing significant numbers of gay men into political and community organizations. It could even be argued that the suffering associated with the disease has helped to create a somewhat different understanding of what it means to be gay. Nonetheless, as one of the main ways of contracting the virus is through sexual contact, and in countries like Britain, through penetrative sex with a man, when HIV/AIDs is diagnosed the infected person, their partner and family are likely to be exposed to the stigma associated with homosexuality as well as with a disease that is associated with pollution (Walker, 1991).

Confusions about the origins of being gay and theories that relate this to parent–child relationships mean that there is a heightened risk of blame and guilt interfering with the ways in which individuals, couples and families come to terms with the diagnosis of HIV/AIDs. In common with many other conditions, during the early stages, it can be difficult to distinguish between indicators of neurological impairment and indicators of the person's emotional state, with families becoming split between defending a psychological or a physical explanation. Where there are unresolved and powerful feeling about the infected person's sexuality, splits that relate to the cause of these symptoms and attitudes towards that person's sexuality can become blurred. Although it tends to become clearer what is physical and what psychological as the disease progresses, people may need help in separating these various layers of experience (Walker, 1991).

Moreover, even if the illness has no obvious connection with sexuality, as, for example, with cancer of the colon or oesophagus, or breast cancer, people who have not identified themselves as gay or lesbian or are not currently in a relationship tend to have a more difficult time. The stigma associated with being gay means that some people feel that the only way of holding on to a positive concept of self and protecting their relationship is to avoid being open about their sexuality with certain people. However, as is the case with all secrets, the pressure to keep this aspect of experience secret can come to consume the relationship, creating a boundary between the secret-bearers and the rest of the world.

Where people have hidden this aspect of their lives from work, and finances are stretched, partners are likely to be unable to take enough time off to take care of a loved one, forcing the ill person to return to the parental home in order to receive the care they need. If the parents do not know their son or daughter is gay, the need to rely on their support may be the catalyst for coming out about their position and/or their relationship. This means that they and their parents are faced with coming to terms with what this information means for themselves and their relationships with one another at the same time as finding out their child has a life-limiting condition (Walker, 1991).

If parents have known and disapproved of their life style, going home can feel like a betrayal of oneself as well as the relationship. Where past differences have led to a 'cut off' with parents and the adult son or daughter has invested all their emotions into their couple relationship, it is not unusual to feel caught in a battle between one's family and partner. However, the experience of caring for one's child at this time and seeing how supportive a child's partner is can help parents become more accepting of their child's sexuality, the relationship, and of themselves.

Being ill when living alone

One of the most notable trends over the past few decades has been the increase in the number of people living in one-person households. For example, in Britain in 2007 over 7 million people were living alone (Office for National Statistics, 2007). Whilst this figure may have reduced as a result of the recent economic crisis, and the figures may be different in other countries, it suggests that a sizeable proportion of people who are ill and disabled live alone, and in many cases are likely to have chosen to do so.

Despite this, relatively little academic attention has been paid to the distinct challenges they face. In common with everyone who becomes seriously ill, people who live alone have to come to terms with the disruptions the illness presents to their anticipated lives, and face similar anxieties about the impact their medical condition might have on their lives, relationships and prospects of employment. However, they are also likely to be faced with challenges that are somewhat different as well. For example, even if people who live alone may have a wide circle of family, friends and colleagues, they are less likely to have access to taken-for-granted practical and emotional support when things are not going well, when they need help in containing their worries and when attending to such basic needs as eating, washing, housework on their own, and collecting medication from the pharmacy, become less feasible. This may account for why research suggests that those who live alone are less likely to be able to remain in the community when they develop a serious and severely debilitating condition, particularly when older (Wenger et al., 1996).

Those who had hoped they would develop a more permanent relationship with a partner may feel that their disability, loss of function, disfigurement and/or risks of becoming pregnant preclude this. The loss of self-esteem that can set in when anyone is ill and more vulnerable can result in avoiding social situations even if one does not live alone. However, in this situation, it limits the possibilities of establishing new relationships even more.

The need for additional care can force people who live alone to become more dependent on their parents or other relatives. Although some may be comfortable with taking this step, where the relationship has been problematic, the dependence and enforced closeness with parents and siblings can feel intolerable. Increased rates of migration may mean that unless they or the rest of the family move, relying on one's family is not feasible when long-term care is required. Moreover, despite the assumption that families pull together at times of crisis, this is not necessarily the case. As such, living alone may be the only way of prioritizing one's own needs.

Although it is important to recognize the need for privacy when working with all ill people who prize their independence, this is particularly important when working with people who have lived alone for much of their lives. It is also important to recognize that concerns about burdening others may mean that they avoid asking for help until this is absolutely imperative, or too late. However, this one aspect of people's lives is unlikely to be the main determinant of how they see themselves and relate to others.

When adults need more intensive support

As discussed previously, faced with illness, disability and the threat of death, many people do not need or want support from outsiders, including members of the medical team. Nonetheless, the challenges discussed above mean that many are likely to benefit from a one-off opportunity to reflect on their experience of being ill. Moreover, where there are particularly difficulties, some will benefit from more intensive support.

For example, I was asked to see Sharon and James, a man in his early forties who had had a second heart attack several months earlier. Although they had been able to support one another during the crisis period, they found themselves at loggerheads once this had abated and James returned to work.

Here too, the work involved listening and bearing witness to their struggles, and introducing questions and ideas that opened up the possibility of seeing things somewhat differently. In common with many couples where one partner has been seriously ill, much of what was said focused on how James should be acting. However, the anger underlying Sharon's comments about James suggested that she felt her own needs were not being met. Therefore, it was important to ask questions that brought both partners' experiences to the fore, as in asking:

- How has your/James's heart attack affected the way in which you see yourself and one another?
- Can you say something about the way in which you might view or experience the issue we are discussing differently from your partner?
- What do you do, James/Sharon, when your partner's guesses about what you want or need do not fit with your own experience?

The work also involved framing some of their struggles as a 'normal' reaction to an abnormal life event, and externalizing (White and Epston, 1990) the challenges the illness had presented to their relationship. For example, instead of speaking about one another as 'having' or 'being the problem', viewing the heart attack as the problem seemed to free them to focus on their shared worries about the future.

The work also included commenting and asking questions that introduced the idea that gender might inform some of the differences in their experiences, responses and expectations of one another: this included reframing James's comment that they had moved into a 'no man's land' as moving into a 'no woman's land' as well. In order to shift their focus away from experiences of illness and care giving, the work also included exploring how they met, what drew them together. This led on to discussing how, because they were at a new phase in their relationship, they might need to learn somewhat different skills (Rolland, 1994).

As is often the case, the work also involved exploring how earlier experiences of relationships might be affecting their responses to situations of illness, loss and caring. What emerged was that because James's father died very young, he believed that he would too. However, he had tended to push himself as far as he could in what seemed to be an attempt to hide his vulnerability from a mother he saw as extremely depressed and needy, and probably from himself. Although he knew this might put him at increased risk, he was desperate to prove he would survive. Sharon's experience was very different: living with a disabled younger brother meant that she was used to putting her own needs second. She had tried to adopt a similar strategy with James, but caring for him seemed to have re-evoked these earlier feelings of resentment, giving rise to 'blow-ups' she found confusing and upsetting.

Although James and Sharon knew something about one another's past, listening to each other reflect on the links between the past and present seemed to lead to a different understanding of their responses. There were still times when Sharon became furious with James because she felt he was taking risks, and James responded by ignoring her, and when his fear of Sharon becoming too needy meant that he withdrew. However, this work helped them redirect some of their anger towards the illness, and confront their shared and very different fears for the future.

Summary

- Adults are more able to offset the stresses of illness and care giving when they have access to a relationship in which they feel listened to and understood, are able to embrace rather than steer clear of the challenges illness and care giving present and are able to see aspects of their experience more clearly.
- When one of them is ill, most couples need to extend their understanding of how much to disclose to one another, and the support they want and are prepared to provide.
- Where the condition affects people's sex lives, it can be extremely helpful to discuss how this aspect of their lives needs to change.
- Gender offers a frame for reflecting on differences that does not position one person as right and the other as wrong.

- Where people have not told their family that they are gay or lesbian, the need for additional care is likely to force them to be more open.
- Although some people who live alone are able to manage on their own when ill, because they are less likely to have automatic access to support, they may be forced to return to their family even if the relationship is uncomfortable.

7

ILLNESS IN LATER LIFE

With the exception of those who live in areas affected by extreme poverty and the HIV/AIDs pandemic, people are living longer and the older population is itself aging (Yancik and Reis, 2000). In the past, 65 was regarded as the point at which people were defined as elderly. However, increased longevity means that it is now more common to think in terms of younger old (65–74), mid-old (75–84) and older old (85 and above) and to regard 75 as the point at which health concerns are likely to be more prevalent (Given et al., 2001).

Despite the fact that older adults tend to have more health concerns, far more attention is paid to the health care of younger and middle generations. There are signs of some shift in practice, as reflected in initiatives aimed at prioritizing older adults and respecting their right to make choices about their care (Department of Health, 2001). Nonetheless, this group of people continue to be offered less access to aggressive forms of treatment or alternative therapies, and receive smaller amounts of pain relief, even when they are being treated for conditions that are more prevalent in later life (Lavelle et al., 2007).

Although the family affect, and are affected by illness in, any one member regardless of their age, this is more pronounced when that person is older. For example, the decision to seek medical help is often precipitated by changes within the family, such as bereavement, retirement, or someone becoming too ill or frail to care for themselves. In addition, because older people are more likely to experience hearing and memory problems than people who are younger, it is often difficult to do an accurate assessment without input from their family or someone who is part of their social network. Moreover, increased frailty, reduced mobility and a restricted social network mean that many older people would have required additional support from their family (particularly daughters) well before deciding to seek medical help (Curtis and Dixon, 2005).

Social attitudes towards aging and illness

The older adults of today have lived through times of enormous upheaval: wars, industrialization, the employment of more women outside of home, greater levels of educational achievement and social mobility, and the impact the increased prevalence of cohabitation, divorce and remarriage have had on family life. Because the older people of today are likely to live longer than their parents, there are few role models to draw on in knowing how to 'do' aging, illness and care giving in later life.

Moreover, particularly in western societies, mandatory retirement and a decline in the roles older people are expected to play mean that rather than being seen as a time of wisdom, old age is more likely to be seen as a time of decline and decay. It is hardly surprising that many older adults report that they feel marginalized, excluded and a nuisance to others (Surbone et al., 2006). This may be why this group of people tend to under-report their symptoms, why health professionals tend to regard symptoms as a 'normal' part of getting older, why depression is often mistaken for confusion, and the frequency with which age is the determining factor in deciding about a person's mental capacities, ability to absorb bad news and wish to be involved in decisions about their care. It may also explain why, in contrast to situations where the ill person is younger, far more academic and clinical attention is paid to the positions of caregivers than to the people entrusted to their care.

Attitudes towards aging appear to be somewhat different in eastern and African societies: older adults tend to be treated with reverence, there is greater respect for their wisdom and depth of experience and greater awareness of what one gains rather than loses as one becomes older. There also tends to be greater acceptance of frailty, and the living body is understood to lose little of its worth when a person becomes cognitively impaired. Nonetheless, the assumptions we have about families tend to lag behind lived experience: although much is made of the burden younger generations face in caring for their parents in western societies, very often older adults take primary responsibility for caring for their loved ones, particularly when others are unable or unwilling to do so. Moreover, increased longevity means that even in African and eastern societies, younger generations are finding the practical and emotional costs of care giving difficult to sustain.

As with younger people, gender appears to inform older adults' experiences and expectations of illness and care. In terms of overall health, illness-related mortality tends to be higher for men, but women are more likely to experience co-morbidity and rate their experience of health lower than the men (Haub, 2007; Waldron, 2005). Women are more likely to be caregivers than men and assume primary care giving responsibilities for their family and friends (Brewer, 2001). However, gendered differences in mortality rates mean that older women are more likely to be receiving that care than is true of men.

While older women tend to look beyond family to other women for psychological support, men are more likely to name their female partners as their main source of support and only confidant. In addition, while women's friendships tend to be organized around self-disclosure and assistance, men's friendships are more likely to be activity orientated. As such, men are at greater risk of becoming isolated when they become increasingly frail.

It has been argued that, because older women tend to have larger social networks, more bonds with friends and siblings and more multiplex ties than men, they are more able to cope with the challenges illness presents (Benbow, 2005). However, factors like gendered inequalities in social positions, unequal distribution of wealth and higher rates of male mortality mean that women are more likely to experience a compromised quality of life as they and their loved ones age (Seale, 1998). In addition, although men appear to be assuming a greater role in caring for vulnerable family members than before, it is still generally true that women spend longer looking after aging parents and caring for dependent children (Adams et al., 2000; Kriseman and Claes, 1997).

Challenges that are distinct to later life

Despite overlaps with the experiences of younger adults, many of the challenges older adults and their families face are distinct (Curtis and Dixon, 2005; Hughes et al., 2009; Surbone et al., 2006). For example, aging tends to affect memory, sleep patterns, digestion, the sensations of sight and hearing, skin, bones and the 'mechanics' of sexual intercourse, all of which can have a profound impact on body image, experiences of self and relationships with others.

As discussed earlier, the almost moral value ascribed to being well and the shame associated with breaching certain social norms mean that people often feel ashamed of the loss of control, helplessness and incapacitation that many medical conditions entail, regardless of their age. However, the neurological impairments can cause memory loss and behaviours that would otherwise be seen as breaching social norms, for example with dementia. This is equally true of other symptoms that are more common in later life, for example incontinence, or being unable to hear or manage one's own affairs. This applies even though, in some cases, symptoms like incontinence may relate to shortfalls in the environment in which the person is being cared for.

Until one's condition deteriorates to the point at which there is little awareness of self and others, these experiences can be deeply embarrassing, giving rise to the belief that whatever one does, it is impossible to defend oneself against the real and imagined disapproval of others. This is likely to be why many older people try to avoid or escape situations in which they are at risk of being exposed, pretend they can hear or remember more than they do, cover up personal responsibility for flaws when they have been exposed, and/or deny their existence (Cheston, 2005).

The hidden nature of shame means that not only is it extremely isolating but it is more difficult for family, friends and professionals to know what is wrong and how to help. Indeed, even if a partner or relative is aware of these difficulties, sensitivity to the person's position tends to mean that they avoid drawing attention to concerns or symptoms that person might find shaming. Moreover, because older adults tend to be on more medication than younger people and often self-medicate, it can be even more difficult to disentangle the physical from the psychological, to know whether greater confusion or memory loss are indicative of deteriorating health or the side effect of their medication.

In addition, older adults are more likely to be dealing with a number of other losses, be this other health concerns or issues that are unrelated such as retirement, reduced finances, the loss of a caregiver role in relation to children, the death of siblings and close friends, having to give up on driving and managing their own finances. Furthermore, many do not have a partner and, when they do, their partner may be too frail to provide the support that is needed. This means that a substantial deterioration in health can result in them and/or their partner having to move into supervised residential care, or becoming increasingly dependent on adult children and other relatives. Just because health concerns are more prevalent in later life and more likely to be accompanied by some level of cognitive deterioration, this does not mean that one's suffering is any less. This is reflected in Long's (1997) account of her father's experience of Alzheimer's disease, in describing his distress on realizing that something was wrong, his ambivalence about seeking help, the relief, despair and denial that set in after the diagnosis, and how he coped as more of his sense of self was chipped away.

It is always difficult to know how much support to offer people who are vulnerable and whether or not to act on their behalf. However, this is more complex in later life. Indeed, as we seem to be living longer and older people tend to have more health concerns that younger people, it is becoming increasingly common for others to take decisions on behalf of older people, including decisions about whether they should be told that their condition is terminal or there are signs of dementia. Although withholding information is likely to be based on the desire to ensure that the person's best interests are held in mind, it undermines their chance of making the most of what they have.

It is obviously impossible to know if the capacity to make rational decisions survives the physical and mental impairment that accompanies some experiences of aging. Nonetheless, believing that this is or is not true has an enormous impact on the ways in which people see themselves and are treated by others. For example, in her analysis of her father's experience of deterioration due to Alzheimer's, Long (1997) found that despite considerable cognitive deficit, his behaviour varied considerably depending on the environments he was in and the way in which he was treated by others.

With this in mind, when working with someone who is unable to talk and it is hard to know what they understand, it is important to try to ascertain whether they can participate in decision making, for example by asking if they would be happy for someone (ourselves, a partner or another family member) to act as their proxy, say what we/they imagine the person might want and let us know through some form of gesture, like an eye blink, whether what is said is an accurate representation of their own position or not (Iveson, 2001).

However, we tend to differ in how much we want to know about and be involved in medical decisions. Moreover, practices which are rooted in the idea of individual responsibility and the individual's right to decide about their care may not fit for people from cultures that place a higher value on a sense of family connectedness and a more interrelated sense of self (Candib, 2002).

It is also important to note that some of the challenges older adults and their families face relate to gaps in service and changes in the wider health care system. For example, as we get older we tend to be at increased risk of developing a stroke, which can result in a permanent or temporary loss of function. Where the level of impairment is considerable, families need time to adjust before being ready to take their relative home. However, the shortage of hospital beds and increased pressure to care for people within the community mean that this is becoming less feasible. Although this is problematic whatever the age of the person, because older adults are less likely to have someone to care for them at home, they and their families are more likely to have to rethink how to ensure they are able to access a greater level of care before they can be discharged.

Challenges to parent–child relationships

Regardless of whether we live together or apart and whether the relationship is supportive or conflicted, the level of identification we have with parents means that parent–child relationships influence understandings of who we are and relationships with others throughout our lives (Rossi and Rossi, 1990). It also means that a parent's deterioration in health is likely to face us with our own sense of frailty and mortality.

When elderly parents become too ill and frail to look after themselves and adult children assume more responsibility for their care, the reversals in role and power that are almost inevitable in these situations may present little difficulty. Where the relationship is conflicted, where adult children have struggled to extricate themselves from their family, and the parent they are caring for was experienced as non-nurturing, absent or even abusive, the enforced closeness and dependency may feel intolerable. However, the experience can also lead to a different appreciation of one another and allow for a sense of companionship that was not possible before.

Even where relationships have been more supportive, the burden on care giving can be enormously stressful. Moreover, because older adults tend to be facing many other losses in their lives, including the death of friends and other relatives, are less mobile than younger people and more likely to be socially isolated, there is a greater risk of their becoming dependent on their children and/or the health care professionals entrusted with their care (Surbone et al., 2006). This is particularly difficult when parents are severely incapacitated; when caring for a parent has had a significant impact on their own finances, adult children have very little respite and continue to be responsible for their own dependent children.

Where there is only one surviving parent, it can be difficult to set limits on providing companionship and care giving because it touches on a fear many of us can empathize with: the fear of dying alone (Rolland, 1994). In some cases, feelings of anger, frustration, guilt and disappointment and unsupported long-term care giving result in what has been called 'elder abuse': in emotional, financial and/or physical abuse. This is more likely when children (or other family carers) feel the person they are looking after takes advantage of them and had been unsupportive to them in the past. However, it is important to bear in mind that the older person may be not only a victim but a perpetrator of abuse (Mouratoglo, 2005).

As such, instead of assuming that because that person is ill and elderly it is too late to address past hurts, it may be impossible for adult children to offer their parent the care they need without discussing the past. Although this can be extremely painful the experience of speaking and being heard can offer both parties some sort of closure, even if it is difficult forgive one another. However, it is important to recognize that the person the adult child wants to be heard by is probably not their vulnerable parent but the person that parent had been before. It is also important to recognize that there may be limits to what people feel able to say or understand and that where the relationship has been extremely abusive, it can be difficult to be in close proximity let alone reach out to one another (Rolland, 1994).

The anticipated loss of a parent moves adult children into the senior position, confronting us with our own aging and sense of mortality (Pipher, 1999; Umberson, 2003). Being faced with parents' vulnerability and the prospect of their death can help siblings set aside past grievances in coming to terms with their shared sense of grief. However, because it also can re-evoke the feelings associated with past rivalries in relation to parents, disagreements about a parent's care can become blurred with feelings that relate to these earlier rivalries. As such, it may be impossible to focus on what parents really need without addressing family-of-origin issues. If this is not feasible, particularly where questions about end of life care and finances are at stake, it is worth exploring whether someone else could negotiate on their behalf.

Challenges to couple relationships

As discussed in relation to younger people, although it can be difficult to deal with the shifts in patterns of power and dependency that tend to arise when one partner's health deteriorates, care giving need not affect the overall satisfaction of the relationship between the ill person and caregiver, and exposure to illness and the threat of death can help partners and/or other family members set aside past differences and develop a closer connection with one another.

However, as older couples are likely to be contending with many other losses in their lives, including retirement, the death of close relatives and colleagues and having to give up one's driving licence and sporting activities, partners might find themselves turning to one another more. Although reduced access to other taken for granted relationships and sources of stimulation can mean that partners look more to one another, resulting in an increased sense of intimacy, the loss of these relationships and sources of stimulation can mean that being there for one another feels stifling. Where childhood experiences of closeness have felt uncomfortable and/or people feel their partner has not been there when they were in need of support before, the enforced closeness and shifts in dependency can re-evoke past feelings of powerlessness and resentments, solidifying earlier feelings of hostility. Moreover, the prevalence of health concerns at this age means that there is an increased risk of health problems and/or caregiver roles becoming a pretext for re-establishing a sense of greater control.

Although much tends to be made of the difficulties couples face when sexual intercourse is more problematic, as discussed earlier sexual intimacy is not always central to partners' relationship with one another, regardless of age. However, because sex can be a way of restoring intimacy in the face of other differences, it may be difficult to discuss relational issues without reference to sex, or resolve differences without finding another way of re-establishing intimacy (Turner, 2005). Whilst older adults may be reluctant to discuss this aspect of their lives, as with younger people, many would benefit from a straightforward discussion about their sex lives. Moreover, although a decline in sexual functioning tends to be seen as a normal consequence of aging, the prevalence of chronic illness in later life means that the decline may be less about aging than ill health (McInnes, 2003).

Memory problems mean that partners often play a key role in monitoring and responding to one another's symptoms. However, where partners feel overburdened and the relationship was difficult before, anger and resentment can interfere with the ability to monitor one another on an accurate and regular basis (Montalvo et al., 1998). Often, it is only when crises arise, for example crises caused by a mismanagement of medication, that adult children (and/or other relatives and friends) become aware of how much their parents are struggling. This lack of awareness may reflect an unconscious desire to deny how their parents' health has deteriorated. However, the desire to avoid being seen as incapable and too needy may mean that parents have hidden the extent of their difficulties from them, particularly where their children's lives represent the fulfilment of their own aspirations (Coles, 2001; Militiades, 2002). If their health or the health of their partner has deteriorated to the level that they are in need of supervised residential care, presenting themselves as managing better than they are may be an attempt to avoid the pain of having to give up their independence, rely more on their children and/or move into residential care.

Intervening at times of difficulty

As with people of all ages, although many older adults and their families are able to cope with the stresses illness presents to their shared and individual lives with relatively little difficulty, others will benefit from additional support from their GP or practice nurse on an occasional basis.

As medical terminology tends to be unfamiliar to most people and it is more difficult to remember what we are told when anxious, sending people a copy of a letter summarizing what the condition entails, the medication that has been prescribed and an explanation of the additional complications that have arisen and can arise is becoming an increasingly accepted aspect of health care. Although a written letter is helpful regardless of one's age, because memory loss tends to increase as we age, this is particularly helpful in later life. As older people are often being cared for by more than one professional as well as members of their family, letters are an effective way of relaying information to others, sharing any additional reflections on the issues that had been raised and limiting the likelihood of further crises developing as a result of misunderstandings (Thorne, 2005).

However, older adults and their family are likely to benefit from more intense psycho-social support where there appear to be high levels of anxiety, hostility and deep despair, where people are unable or unwilling to hear one another, resolve conflicts and reach decisions about care, where the family patterns are chaotic or overly rigid and where there is a level of closeness that does not allow the ill person (or other family members) to experience some sense of autonomy.

Regardless of whether people are seen in counselling sessions or as part of a medical consultation, as the family is likely to play a pivotal role in older adults' experience of illness, rather than focusing purely on the individual in question or their main carer, it is important to take account of the ways in which their experiences affect and are affected by their relationship with one another, as well as relationships with the rest of the family. Where the ill person is cared for by a combination of family, professional and/or paid carers it is also important to pay attention to the relationships between that person, their family and others entrusted with their care. Indeed, because co-morbidity is more prevalent when older, and people are likely to be treated by more than one health care professional, in some situations, instead of offering a person or family additional support, what may be more important is helping the professionals find a different way of communicating and working together.

Fear of therapy and ambivalence about change mean that people of all ages often delay seeking psychological help until they are at breaking point. However, because today's older people tend to be less familiar with therapy, are more likely to regard the need for psychological assistance as an indication of madness and to be sceptical about the value of talking about problems, this is more likely in later life. As such, it is even more important to adopt a gentle and collaborative approach and pay particular attention to establishing a sense of trust than when working with people who are younger.

Couples who have been in conflict for a long time tend to be more resistant to change. As such, when difficulties arise, we may need to work more strategically. For example, encouraging partners to spend more time apart can have the paradoxical effect of increasing their awareness of what they do offer one another and a greater desire to be together (Iveson, 2001).

Although it is important to avoid viewing age as the only determinant of how people respond, and making assumptions on the basis of age, older adults are often more comfortable with talking about specific behaviours than feelings and have reservations about being understood by someone who is younger. They are also more likely to be faced with a shorter concentration span, memory loss and certain levels of sensory impairment. Therefore, we may need to change how we interact, for example by speaking more slowly, making sure we are facing the person or people concerned (particularly where there is hearing loss), touching their arm to attract attention when concentration seems to flag, offering briefer sessions and providing a pad for taking notes (Miller et al., 1997).

As experiences of illness can feel shaming and older adults are more likely to feel marginalized, it is important to create a space in which people feel able to express how they feel, reflect on their experience and mourn for what has been lost. Where their stories are dominated by feelings of blame and resentment, it is also important to work towards helping them construct a less pathologizing understanding of their experience and, where feasible, look for alternative ways of responding. Exploring the circumstances that surround issues they find particularly difficult can bring the interactional nature of these experiences to the fore so that it becomes more possible to think about what needs to change to repair and avoid these difficulties escalating further.

As with younger people, where much of what is said is expressed in terms of 'I', it can be helpful to work towards establishing a greater sense of mutuality and reframing what is presented as right and wrong as different but no less 'right' or well-intended. In contrast, where what is said is expressed primarily in terms of 'we' but one person's views seem to dominate, it can be helpful to ask questions that draw attention to differences. Indeed, helping people appreciate that the views we hold are informed by a range of factors (for example gender) is often the most important step towards enabling them to speak more openly and hear one another.

Externalizing, framing health concerns and physical symptoms as external to the person rather than integral to who they are, can be particularly helpful where the condition has resulted in cognitive deficit and personality change: it enables the family to direct negative feelings towards the disease rather than the person concerned, and if they are sufficiently aware, provides the sufferer and the rest of the family some relief from the idea they are acting in an inappropriate or hurtful way intentionally. Framing some of the emotions evoked by caring for and being cared for at this stage of life as a 'normal' response to extremely challenging circumstances rather than a sign of personal failure can have a similarly de-pathologizing effect: instead of blaming the sufferer, it becomes more possible to view the disease as taking the person they knew away from them, destroying their relationship with one another, and to focus on how to prevent this dominating their lives (Mouratoglou, 2005).

Genograms and life-story work can be extremely helpful, particularly where the older person moves into residential care. As older adults tend to have thick files, genograms are a way of collating and summarizing the most pertinent relationships and changes in the life course. However, as discussed before, genograms can also be a powerful therapeutic tool: they help to position personal experience as part of the wider pattern that involves others, bringing wider family relationships and life-cycle issues to the fore (Stockwell, 2005). Where the person who is unwell is cognitively impaired or unable to speak, engaging their relatives in this process helps to remind the person, their family and the professionals responsible for their care that their life has not only been about illness and incapacity, limiting the potential to objectify that person.

Unsupported, ongoing care giving can rob an elderly relative of dignity and overburden adult children who have considerable childcare and career commitments. With this in mind, where a partner, parent or another relative provides long-term care, it is important to explore the possibilities of substitute care. In addition to offering respite, it offers the carer increased involvement with the outside world and in so doing brings conversations about issues other than illness into the home, all of which tends to increase the likelihood of feeling able to care for the affected person at home (Rolland, 1994).

Where caring has become a central aspect of the person's identity and the need for additional support is seen as a failure, partners and adult children may need the permission of the person who is ill before feeling able to engage (or re-engage) with a life that is only about caring. However, others may find it difficult to accept such respite unless they feel it is in the best interests of the person they are caring after.

Practical constraints and earlier relational difficulties mean that it is sometimes preferable for people to be seen on their own. Because experiences of care giving and illness can be lonely as well as frightening, it can be helpful to be offered a chance to meet with others who are in a similar position (be this other carers or older people who are ill). As discussed previously, meeting others offers people an opportunity to learn from the experience of others affected by similar circumstances, including gaining practical ideas of how to negotiate with professionals to ensure that they and their loved ones receive the support that is needed (Cameron, 2005).

Transitions to residential care

The stresses and strains of long-term care mean that, particularly in the west, respite or permanent residential care is an option families may consider as the disease progresses and the need for care becomes more demanding (Davies and Nolan, 2003; Long, 1997).

Where residential care is seen as culturally inappropriate, is poor in quality and where the family's finances and/or additional state support allows for this, one of the other ways of meeting the needs of increasingly frail older adults is by recruiting the services of additional professional and domestic workers. The availability of affordable domestic labour increases the possibilities of older adults being able to continue living at home, close to people and places that are familiar. The combination of additional professional and paid help can go a long way towards ensuring that people receive the care they need. However, when younger relatives (particularly children) live elsewhere, it is rarely able to make up for the isolation that becoming ill and increasingly frail tends to present. Moreover, in these circumstances relatives or someone else need to keep a close eye on how that person is doing and the quality of care they are receiving.

Every transition begins with an ending. By their very nature transitions involve ambiguity: letting go of what was and moving forward. Moving to residential care can lead to improved physical and psychological wellbeing and increased access to social support. This is more likely to be true when people have been finding it difficult to cope on their own and relationships with family or paid carers have become fraught. However, the loss of one's own home, friends and familiar surroundings can lead to a profound sense of abandonment and disorientation, leading to deterioration in physical as well as emotional well-being. A decision to seek residential care is usually taken at a point when living independently has become too stressful, the level of care that is needed stretches family, friends, professionals and/or paid carers beyond what is tolerable and/or does not provide enough of a safety net to avoid health crises escalating.

However, residential care runs counter to the notions of relational care and family support many people hold dear. Where the decision relates to a parent, parents have to reconcile themselves with being unable to receive the sort of care they had imagined their children would have been able to provide, and children with being unable to meet their parents' and their own expectations of what family care and filial responsibility means. One of the other difficulties is that residential care is often only considered after a blow-up or a significant gap in care has resulted in a series of health crises. As such, families are likely to be at breaking point, overwhelmed by loss, failure and disloyalty, and anxious about how they and their loved one will cope once an admission has taken place. Moreover, as discussed previously, the identifications children have with parents mean that the move to residential care tends to confront them with a sense of their own vulnerability and mortality.

Coming to such a decision is particularly difficult where family members cannot agree on the best course of action and the facilities that are available are regarded as unsatisfactory. As some of these differences may be based on insufficient information, it is becoming common practice to invite families to meet members of staff to clarify the services that are available, explore the older relative's current needs and develop more realistic long-term care plans. This helps to ensure that everyone is clear about what is expected, the institutional facilities and restrictions, how much time they can spend together and who to call when they are unsure of what to do.

As it can be difficult to reach such decisions, it is important to ensure that families have access to non-intrusive and non-judgemental support. Professionals have enormous potential to influence people's experience of whether they are acting in the best interest of their relative (Davies and Nolan, 2003). Because the boundary between professionals and family members tends to be particularly ambiguous at points of transition, we need to be mindful of stepping in too far, of pushing people into decisions they are not ready to make, and helping families hold on to the sort of care and support they can still offer one another.

Once a decision is taken to go ahead, it is important to encourage the family, particularly the main caregiver, to build relationships with the staff that are based on equality, collaboration and clearly delineated roles. The sense of loss that tends to prevail at such times means that families are likely to benefit from the chance of engaging in growth-inducing activities in order to balance the difficulties they are experiencing (Caron, 1997). This could include collaborating in compiling a memory box, book, photo album, poems or music they had loved, as reminders of the richness of a life that was less dominated by illness, disability and care giving.

Although we tend reflect on the ways in which we have lived throughout our lives, this is more common when older (Butler et al., 1991). As such, genogram work can be extremely helpful too. Discussions about the past can mean that younger generations learn aspects about their relative and their family they were unaware of. Moreover, because we tend to retain more of our long-term memory when more recent memories are hard to hold on to, talking about the past is likely to be affirming to the older person as well. The other advantage is that where everyone in the family agrees, sharing some of these stories with the care staff can help to ensure that those entrusted with caring for their loved one have a greater understanding of their earlier life. This is likely to be particularly helpful where the condition has resulted in a significant deterioration in the person's mental capacities.

Finally, the identifications professionals have with their own parents mean that the boundary between the personal and professional can easily be blurred when working with older adults, particularly when working with people in an ongoing capacity, as with residential care. As such, we find ourselves acting more like a daughter (or son) than a health professional, or the reverse, adopting a particularly distant approach to negate the risks of identifying too closely. However, as discussed in relation to other aspects of identity, including gender, racialization and culture, there is a fine line between respecting an older adult's greater life experiences and becoming overly organized by differences in age (Curtis and Dixon, 2005).

Summary

- Although people seem to be living longer and older adults tend to have more health concerns, they tend to be offered less access to aggressive forms of treatment and alternative therapies and receive smaller amounts of pain relief.

- Older adults who become increasingly ill and frail tend to be dealing with other losses as well, including the death of friends and the loss of employment.
- Although caring for an elderly partner or parents can be deeply satisfying and help in healing past rifts, long-term care giving can be difficult to sustain.
- Where some members of the family feel it is impossible for the older person to manage on their own, this could result in their taking more responsibility for their care or suggesting a move into residential care.
- Where differences in views about the care of an older relative become entangled with differences that relate to other aspects of their relationship, families are likely to benefit from additional support.
- Because older people tend to be more sceptical about talking about problems and are more likely to have a shorter concentration span, memory loss and certain levels of sensory impairment than others, we may need to change our usual style of interacting.
- However, there is a fine line between respecting what is different and becoming overly organized around age.

8

DEATH, BEREAVEMENT AND LIVING BEYOND LOSS

Across the generations and in every culture, individuals, families and communities have had to find ways of coming to terms with death (Walsh, 2004). Although this is a deeply personal process, the death or threatened death of someone who has played a significant role in our life tends to be bound up with many other experiences of loss, for example, in the case of a life-long partner, with the loss of that relationship, a certain set of roles, and the loss of the shared future that might have been. As such, it sets off a series of shock waves that reverberate throughout the family immediately as well as long after the death or threatened death.

Freud (1917) drew attention to the relational consequences of death in suggesting that when we love, we incorporate aspects of the 'other' into our ego. This means that when we lose someone we love it is as if a part of ourselves has died. It may account for why, even though the death of a parent in our middle and later years is far more anticipated than a death that takes place when we are younger, it tends to be one of the most profound emotional, psychological and social points in our lives, regardless of how old we are.

Kubler-Ross's (1970) model of grieving has had a considerable impact on constructions of loss, namely that over time we tend to move from denial, anger, bargaining, depression to some sense of acceptance. Her work led to greater awareness of the fact that mourning is a process that unfolds over time, a life-long adjustment to a world without the deceased. However, as discussed before, the idea of a universal stage-based model fails to take account of the variability of human responses: that many people oscillate between intense sadness and despair, pining, resigned acceptance and periods in which it is more possible to re-engage with a changed world.

Her work led to greater awareness of the beneficial effects of expressing how we feel on being able to mourn and let go (Parkes, 1971, 2002; Vaughan-Cole, 2006). However, some of the thoughts and feelings evoked at times of death are too frightening or shameful to acknowledge to oneself, let alone others. Moreover, some of these thoughts may feel too special and private to share with others as they embody memories of who the deceased was and our relationship with them. A number of factors appear to inform the ways in which we come to terms with death, namely:

- The manner of the death, for example whether the death was sudden or lingering, expected or came about as a result of a violent incident, and whether the circumstances of death alienate people from their social network, as when the condition is linked with alcohol, drug abuse, or the deceased committed suicide.
- The relationship between the dying and their family around the time of death.
- The meaning of the death in terms of the family life cycle.
- The ability and readiness of the dying and their family to express their grief to others.
- Family histories of loss and the presence of other sources of stress.
- Socio-cultural beliefs about death, an afterlife and the disease in question.

Nonetheless, in all contexts of death, families tend to be faced with four main tasks (Walsh and McGoldrick, 2004):

- Coming to a shared acknowledgment of the reality of death.
- Sharing aspects of their experience of loss with one another.
- Re-organizing the family system, re-establishing some sense of equilibrium and reworking past patterns of relating.
- Reinvesting in other relationships and pursuits in life.

On moving from curative to palliative care

Advances in care mean that far more people who are seriously ill and would previously have died are able to live relatively normal lives. They have also meant that it is more possible to keep people alive with the aid of life-supporting equipment. As the condition becomes more advanced and treatment is no longer effective, death may be sudden. Where this is not the case and the person who is clearly dying is suffering, the individual, family and professionals may be faced with deciding whether or not to shift the focus from curative to palliative care. However, reaching such a decision can be extremely difficult as it raises profound relational, ethical and legal questions for professionals and families alike.

For example, Nina, a woman in her late seventies who was in end-stage renal failure, was admitted to hospital when her health deteriorated to a point where her family felt unable to care for her at home. When admitted she came across as coherent and as having a good sense of humour. However, to the careful observer she showed signs of helplessness, fear and confusion, and her behaviour was somewhat disinhibited. At first Nina believed she would be going home, but when naso-gastric tubes were fitted and the treatment became more intrusive, she began to slide downhill, physically as well as emotionally.

Although she continued to ask to go home and seemed to be mystified by her lack of recovery, neither her family nor the professionals seemed to have the language or felt able to tell her she was dying. It was only once her condition had deteriorated further that the possibility of withdrawing treatment was considered and the work began to focus on helping her and her family understand that she would not recover. However, by then, Nina was too distraught, unwell and confused to be able to communicate with her family. In the end her family felt let down by the hospital, and they and the professionals remained deeply troubled by the circumstances of her death.

The nursing staff were used to working with people who were dying. However, they felt so uncomfortable about the way in which this death had been managed, that a meeting was set up to help them debrief. At that meeting, the discussion focused on what was particular about her situation, and whether a change in plan could have been reached earlier that could have made it more possible for Nina and her family to face the reality of her death together, and the staff to feel more at peace with the care they were able to provide.

The palliative care movement arose out of a desire to prevent situations like this arising. Although it came about as a response to terminal cancer, the ideals embodied in palliative care have been extended to other situations in which the major emphasis of care is on alleviating the suffering of those who are dying as well as on the treatment of the side affects of certain curative treatments. Rather than working towards a cure, emphasis is placed on managing pain and other physical symptoms and ensuring that dying patients and their families receive as high a standard of care as possible in the last few days.

Palliative care is based on a commitment to improve 'the quality of life of patients and their families facing the problems associated with life-threatening illness, through the prevention and relief of suffering by means of early identification and impeccable assessment and treatment of pain and other problems, physical, psychosocial and spiritual' (World Health Organization, 2010). Indeed, one of the central tenets of palliative care is that in itself death is not a failure: death is only a failure if it is not as restful and dignified as it could be. This means ensuring that:

- People have access to physical comfort and emotional support.
- The dying person is treated with respect.
- Information and emotional support are provided to family members.
- The care people receive is well co-ordinated.
- There is an absence of avoidable suffering consistent with clinical, ethical and cultural standards.
- The individual and their family are offered space to reflect on the decisions they need to take, and where there are significant differences in opinion, reach some form of reconciliation.

To provide this sort of care, it is important to ensure that there are pre-set but flexible pathways of care for the dying, advanced care planning, regular mechanisms for feedback with families and legal clarity about the patient's ability to reach an informed choice about their care. It is also important to respect the cultural, spiritual and philosophical values of the people with whom one is working and ensure that there are opportunities to explore what the patient and their family have been told, understand and need clarified.

The British Mental Capacity Act of 2005 enshrined the individual's right to refuse medical treatment and/or artificial ventilation in advance to ensure that their wishes are known should they lose the capacity to express themselves in the future. However, as reflected in the number of high profile court cases and media attention this aspect of health care receives, translating this into practice is complicated.

Interestingly, one seldom hears of opposition with respect to withdrawing or non-initiation of certain forms of treatment, for example with renal dialysis. This means that within the field of renal failure, significant numbers of people die following withdrawal or non-initiation of dialysis. As a result, provided death is not sudden and cognitive functioning remains intact, people have a chance of taking control over their final weeks and months, closing their affairs and saying goodbye (Moss et al., 2004).

Nonetheless, because withholding or withdrawing treatment touches on profound ethical, relational and legal issues, reaching such a decision is never easy, even when brain stem cell death has been diagnosed (Long et al., 2008). This tends to be particularly complicated when people are too unwell to express their view. To limit the chances of this situation arising, it has been suggested that general practitioners explore what people who are well, particularly older people, might want in the event of becoming increasingly ill. This includes establishing whether they would want to know the name and details of any condition they are diagnosed with, who they would want help from in reaching decisions about their health, and whether they would want doctors to do everything to keep them alive, or place greater emphasis on making them as comfortable as possible (Candib, 2002).

However, as helpful as such conversations might be, one needs to be extremely careful to ensure that the intentions that lie beneath these conversations are not misunderstood. This is particularly important when age, ethnicity, racialization and socio-economic factors mean that they have not, or feel that they have not, been able to access good enough care. Although it is often assumed that older people do not want to talk about death, the opposite appears to be true: older people are often less fearful of death than younger people and are not only willing but welcome the opportunity to talk about death and their end-of-life wishes (Anderson, 1997).

Even when the person's wishes are known, reaching a decision to withdraw or withhold treatment can be extremely difficult for families: the prospect of death tends to trigger feelings that belong to the past so that it may feel impossible to separate feelings about what is in the best interests of a relative from feelings that relate to other aspects of the relationship. This is particularly important to bear in mind when the dying person is a parent and was seen to have held the family together, and in the case of transnational families their death represents a more final split from one's culture and country of origin (Altschuler, 2008; Falicov, 1998). Consequently, it is important to ensure that families have the space to discuss their dilemmas carefully and are given the medical and legal information they need in order to come to a shared decision.

Reaching such a decision can be extremely difficult for professionals as well, because it goes against the aspirations that are likely to have brought them into this work, the desire to heal others. Moreover, the close bonds that tend to develop between someone who is extremely ill, their family and the professionals mean that the death of a person entrusted to one's care represents a very real loss to the professionals as well. As such, it may be difficult to separate one's own feelings from the feelings of the family concerned.

Provided the adult who is dying is able to comprehend what is happening, they, their physicians and family are responsible for weighing up the practical and emotional benefits and costs of additional intervention against the possibility of ending their lives. However, when the person concerned is a child, although it is essential to take account of their views, parents and physicians take primary responsibility for these decisions (Christ, 2000; Field and Behrman, 2003). Moreover, although it is important to engage with the rest of the family whatever the dying person's age, it is particularly important when a child is dying: because there are often other children living in their home, parents and children may need help in disentangling feelings that relate to their own experience from those of one another. Furthermore the likelihood of personal resonance is higher when children are involved (Wilson, 2005).

However, as discussed in the next chapter, it is also important to recognize that the beliefs we have about end-of-life care might differ from those of the families concerned. For example, when working with people with a cultural background that is different from our own, common areas of difference include beliefs about the individual's right to information and right to decide about their care, the value of truth-telling, and the notion of an afterlife. Nonetheless, even if we are from the same background, our ideas about end-of-life care may be very different.

Helping families mourn and move on

As discussed in relation to living with a life-limiting illness, although many people are able and prefer to deal with their grief without the assistance of professionals, others will benefit from additional support. However, it can be difficult to know when this is needed because it is not clear what 'recovering' from grief means, how long this 'should' take and whether it is ever possible to recover from certain forms of loss, such as the death of a child (Brennan and Moynihan, 2004; Walsh and McGoldrick, 2004). Nonetheless, additional support is likely to be required when, after a few months, the bereaved are unable to experience moments that are free from intense distress, feel pleasure without guilt, focus some of their energy on everyday living rather than being totally preoccupied with loss, and function in their social role, for example as a partner, parent, employee and member of the community (Weiss, 1993).

In some cases the person who is dying is more ready to acknowledge the terminal nature of their condition and in others the rest of the family is more ready to do so. In either case, this need not reflect a 'real' not knowing but fear about the effects acknowledging this might have on themselves and others, and/or an unwillingness to confront what is known at this precise time or in the presence of particular people (Fredman, 1997; Shotter, 1994). Nonetheless, failing to acknowledge that the end is near limits the chance of putting one's affairs in order and having the sorts of conversations many would want before saying goodbye. In some cases, it is left to an outsider, a professional, a member of the extended family or a friend to help the family, or some parts of the family, face their own reality and grieve.

Regardless of whether we meet people on a one-off or more ongoing basis, probably the most valuable input we have to offer at such times is our presence: listening and bearing witness to the distress, pain and confusion they are experiencing (Anderson, 1997; Meyerstein, 1994). However, it is also important to normalize the complicated feelings exposure to death tends to arouse. When stories people share are at odds with the emotions their facial expression portrays, and in the case of children, with images portrayed in their play and drawings, it can be helpful to draw attention to this mismatch in order to help people speak more openly.

However, responses to death tend to be informed by deep-seated beliefs. Suggesting that it is helpful to speak more openly to children when this contradicts someone's own belief can be experienced as an attack on their beliefs or an attack on their relationship with the deceased. Consequently, although it can be helpful to share research findings and what we have learned from clinical experience, it is important to respect and engage with people's beliefs before attempting to explore how they fit with their actual experience.

Where parents know they are dying and there are young children, memory boxes and books can be used as a way of collating information that will be important for the future, for example, a power of attorney that stipulates parents' end-of-life wishes, funeral plans, wills, who they would like to look after their children in the future, information about key people and events in their lives and the lives of their children. It can be useful to gather together items that will help their children hold on to (and in the case of younger children, develop an intimate understanding of) their parent and/or a reminder about aspects of their lives that were not dominated by illness, for example photographs, poems or music parents feel their children would enjoy when there are older. This is particularly important when children are very young at the time of death and the final months have been extremely harrowing.

Mourning is also likely to be more complicated when the grief that one feels is disenfranchised, when it relates to 'a loss that is not or cannot be openly acknowledged, publicly mourned, or socially supported' (Doka, 1999: 37). Where the death relates to a stigmatized condition like HIV/AIDs, collating items and information that reflect other aspects of their lives and keeping them in a safe place, for example a specially decorated memory box, offers parents a way of helping their children establish a wider image of who they were, limiting the loss and confusion children experience when they have very little information about their deceased parents or knowledge about their earlier life and origins. Memory boxes could include anything from compact discs of one's favourite music, bus tickets of journeys taken together, shells from holidays at the beach or petals and, as smell can be a powerful way of triggering memories, a bottle of perfume or aftershave.

Memory boxes are also being used to help people affected by the HIV/AIDs virus live positively, and hold on to and even celebrate life. Whilst decisions about what to include are deeply personal, sharing some of this experience with people with whom one is intimately connected, or others with the same condition, can go a long way towards normalizing one's experience and coming to terms with the anticipated loss (Morgan, 2001).

Where the condition has been long term and/or when the condition has resulted in cognitive damage (as with Alzheimer's and other forms of dementia) the burden of care giving may mean that death feels like such a relief that it is impossible to mourn until more time has passed (Anderson, 1997; Stockwell, 2005). As discussed in the previous chapter, constructing a family genogram can help survivors reconnect with these aspects of their lives, recognize their anger and disappointment about the way in which the condition seemed to have 'stolen' their partner, parent or sibling and acknowledge the mixture of relief and loss they feel. In other cases, although others view the death as a merciful release, this is not the way the surviving partner, children or siblings feel. Indeed, where death frees survivors to 'reclaim' earlier memories of their loved one, survivors are likely to be faced with mourning the past that might have been as well as the loss of a shared future.

The loss of a loved one can open up, and/or give people the courage to try to make sense of, troubling feelings that pre-date illness and death. Because most bereavement services are too stretched to take on the long-term work, a decision may be taken to refer relatives on to another agency. However, as it can be difficult for people who are facing so much loss in their life to be told they are being referred on to someone else, it is important to prepare them for this change, discuss what can and cannot be shared with another professional and reflect on what this ending means for the bereaved as well as ourselves. Indeed, discussions about ending the relationship with a professional can allow for discussions about the loss of a loved one that have not seemed possible before.

In some cases, discomfort about the way in which a loved one died means that grieving relatives prefer to seek help from an outside agency. For example, Annabelle, a woman in her late thirties, sought help several months after her mother died in relation to an aspect of disenfranchised grief (Doka, 1999) that has as yet received limited attention: the difficulties of mourning and letting go when a parent, child or sibling with a progressively debilitating condition decides to end their life. Her mother decided to end her life when her Parkinson's disease had deteriorated to a point where it was clear that she would need twenty-four-hour care. Although she had told her partner and a close friend, she had not told Annabelle and the rest of her children.

In listening to Annabelle, what became apparent as that although she had tried to get on with her life as before, there were days when she felt unable to get out of bed, go to work and relate to others. It also became apparent that she found it difficult to discuss her mother or share how she felt with the rest of her family because they thought it was wrong to be angry and regret what her mother had done, as she had the right to make her own decision about how and when to die. It also became apparent that she thought her partner or friends would not understand how she felt and was afraid of becoming an object of curiosity. However, she also held back from turning to them because she felt she did not deserve their support, as she had realized the depths of her mother's suffering and had not been able to persuade her to change her mind.

With this in mind, an important aspect of the work involved trying to help Annabelle separate her feelings of grief from feelings that related to the circumstances of her mother's death. This included encouraging her to reflect on her experience, normalizing some of the complicated feelings survivors often experience following the suicide of a close relative or friend. It also involved focusing on her mother's experience of Parkinson's, asking her to imagine how she might have felt had she been in her mother's position as well as exploring how other aspects of their relationship might be affecting the way she was feeling.

Child and adolescent bereavement

Although the loss of someone we love during childhood or adolescence is relatively rare, it is an experience roughly 5% of children and adolescents under 15 are likely to face (Currier et al., 2007). Where the process of mourning is more complicated, as, for example, when the circumstances of death are traumatic, there is an increased risk of developing subsequent mental health problems. However, when children and adolescents receive the support they need, this is not the case. Nonetheless, even where children seem to have moved on with their lives, feelings of loss tend to re-emerge at significant stages in their lives (Christ, 2000). For example, girls whose mothers have died often feel a renewed sense of loss when they reach puberty and, in common with boys, when they leave school, choose a career or become parents.

However, children's concept and experience of death appears to be somewhat different from that of adults (Bluebond-Langer, 1978). Although children who have been seriously ill and are dying tend to develop an understanding far earlier that death is final and cannot be reversed, more usually it is only between the ages of 5 and 8 that they begin to understand the finality of death (Lansdown and Benjamin, 1985; Slaughter and Griffiths, 2007). Many adults may oscillate between periods of sadness and periods when it is more possible to get on with their life. However, the tendency to oscillate from one end of the spectrum to the other is more pronounced with children. Indeed, in a booklet discussing children's experience of death and bereavement, Winston's Wish (2000) states that it is as if children are able to skip along in the sunshine at one moment but find themselves waist-deep in a 'muddle' or 'puddle' of grief at the next.

Moreover, the importance of parent–child relationships to both parties means that it can be difficult for parents to disentangle their own grief from that of a child. As such, they are likely to benefit from a chance to talk about the death and ways of helping children come to terms with the changes in their lives (Beale et al., 2004). It is also helpful to offer parents and other carers suggestions of books to read with children and guidelines on how to talk about death. Although the needs of each child will vary, in general, this includes suggesting parents:

- Talk with and listen to the thoughts and concerns their children have.
- Answer questions as truthfully as possible.

- Provide information about death and grief as a way of addressing the distortions that can arise from what others say, their developmental stage and magical thinking.
- Use simple terms to explain death rather than trying to soften the blow.
- Avoid using explanations that are confusing or likely to increase their fears (for example, saying the deceased is 'asleep').
- Acknowledge when one does not know the answer.
- Allow children to participate in marking the death and remembering the deceased.
- Recognize and affirm their feelings as well as one's own.
- Reassure them of the normalcy of the feelings exposure to death can evoke.
- Talk about the person who died.
- Maintain as much of their usual activities as possible but allow some respite when needed.
- Keep the school informed.

Where a parent or sibling has died it can feel extremely difficult to know how to answer such questions as 'Why did this happen?', 'Will you (mummy or daddy) or I die too?' and 'Will I get another mummy/daddy?' Although it is understandable that there will be times when adults feel a need to act as a protective filter, it is preferable to answer their questions as truthfully as possible and, where the person who died was a young parent or sibling, stress how unusual it is to die at that stage of life.

However, many adults, be they parents, grandparents, other relatives or professionals find it painful to acknowledge the intensity of a child's grief. With this in mind, it can be helpful to share some of the different ways in which children respond: for example that some tend to become stuck in survival mode, try to hide or deny how they feel, distract parents when they seem particularly distressed by acting in a caring or even aggressive way, display phobic symptoms and become fearful of entering a room or touching anything they associate with the deceased, or show their distress through somatic complaints.

It is also useful to share that younger children often regress, becoming more dependent on parents (or in the case of parental death on their surviving parent or another relative), more fearful of sleeping alone, lose interest in friends and their usual activities, display physical symptoms, worries about their health and become more anxious about going to school. It is also not unusual for children to have intrusive thoughts about the person who died and the circumstances of their death, to think that they are to blame or become afraid that they or their parents will die too. However, in most cases, this is short lived and children who are well supported and able to make sense of their own experience of grief are able to regain their confidence and trust in their world.

Experiences of bereavement can be enormously isolating. With this in mind, a growing number of palliative care centres run bereavement groups for children and adolescents following the death of a close relative, as well as groups for their parents and other carers. As discussed in relation to illness, group sessions offer people an opportunity to meet others who are in the same position and in this case to ask questions about death and dying, share memories of the deceased, draw on the experiences of others and learn new ways of expressing how they feel (Way et al., 2010).

Where the person who has died is the child's parent, parenting groups offer surviving parents a chance to reflect on the challenges of stepping into the shoes of the deceased, the impact growing up in a household without a male or female parent figure might have on their children and the challenges this is likely to present. For example, where the child's father has died and there are sons, mothers are likely to benefit from a chance of discussing the questions they have about bringing up a son without access to a male model, including how to respond to challenging aggressive behaviour. Similarly, where a mother dies, fathers are likely to benefit from discussing the concerns they have about bringing up daughters, such as concerns about the sorts of discussions that will be needed when they reach puberty.

However, some children need more intensive support. In working with children and their families at such times, as discussed earlier, it is important to relate at a level they understand and engage with the imaginative world of play. This means providing access to age-appropriate toys and drawing materials that allow the possibility of working through and sharing some of their concerns through play, as well as books that open up the possibility of discussing illness, death and loss (Carol, 1995).

This is reflected in Way and Bremner's (2010) description of their work with Junior, a 6-year-old boy who had become increasingly aggressive at school; this involved using a book from a series they thought he would be familiar with (the Mister Men Series) to help him and his parents talk about the death of his older brother. For example, they asked Junior who his favourite Mr Men character was (in this case, Mr Tickle) before moving on to 'wonder' aloud whether there were times when other characters like Mr Angry, Mr Punch and Mr Temper tried to egg him on to do things that upset his school friends and teacher, getting him into trouble and spoiling his life.

The idea of engaging at the level of the child and drawing on the imagination is also reflected in Wilson's (2005) work with 5-year-old Alan, whose only sibling, a sister, died before he was born, and who, like Junior, had become increasingly aggressive at school. On meeting Alan, Wilson noticed something that his parents had not mentioned in their earlier meeting: how sad their son seemed to be. Inviting the parents to observe their son's play through a one-way screen helped them recognize their son's sadness. Wilson reframed this sadness by suggesting that Alan had lost his smile, and encouraging him and his parents to imagine where he left his smile, where it could be found, why his smile had been lost and whether there were times when anyone else in the family felt sad. This helped his parents recognize their need to talk with their son about his sister, his need for fun and that it was time for them to let go of some of their grief.

Other ways of helping children express how they feel include using a toy to 'voice' what we guess they are thinking and feeling. This allows us to draw on work with other bereaved children as well as our own experiences of bereavement in normalizing the thoughts and feelings that can arise. However, it is important to make it clear that what we say might not fit for them and to ask them to let us know when the comments of the toy do or do not accord with the way in which they see things.

Children, particularly those who are younger, tend to find it easier to talk about the deceased and ask questions when engaged in an activity. One such activity involves decorating a stone in a way that says something about their relationship with the person who died. Stones can also be used to help children reflect on the bad as well as the good times, as in offering the child a chance to decorate or play with stones that are rough as well as smooth.

Workbooks and activity sheets designed with experiences of loss in mind can be particularly useful. Examples include worksheets that are pre-marked with faces or animals that depict a wide range of emotions; pages that contain incomplete sentences like 'things that make me happy (sad or angry) …'; pages entitled 'my family' or 'special memories'; and columns entitled 'before' (mummy, daddy or another close relative died), 'during' (the time of their death) and 'after' the death. Children's responses tend to offer insight into the ways in which the rest of the family is managing as well as themselves. For example, where a child does not know how to respond to a question that relates to 'before' their parent died, this might mean that they were too young to remember that parent and/or that the horror of seeing their health deteriorate wiped out any memories of what life was like before. It may also mean that the rest of their family have been unable or unwilling to talk about the deceased. In these situations they may need help in building and holding on to more positive memories of the deceased. Many are afraid of their memories fading and do not know whether the deceased and their memories of the deceased will be, and are allowed to continue to be, part of their lives.

With this in mind, as discussed in relation to parents, it can be helpful to suggest that they keep things that are connected to the deceased in a special place, a 'memory box' which can be added to and shown to others when and if they would like to. Depending on the age of the child, they may prefer to do this on their own or with help from an adult, for example, in the case of parental death, from the other parent, a grandparent or friend of the family. Those who were too young when the person died, or had lived apart from the deceased, may need to draw on the memories of people who knew the deceased better. Another way of sharing stories about the deceased is to suggest the family work together to construct a genogram that depicts those who have died as well as those who are alive. Working on genograms together can offer insight into the ways in which parents and children share stories with one another, what children know about the deceased, and the events associated with their death.

Since so much of their lives tends to be disrupted following the death of someone close to them, where children are struggling it is also useful to explore what else is happening to them, including changes in who takes them to school, changes in schooling and housing, as well as asking about some of the good things that are happening (Way and Bremner, 2010).

Attending to grief at school

Worries about surviving relatives, fears about breaking down in front of their friends and uncertainty about what their teachers and peers know mean that returning to school after a close relative has died can be extremely complicated. However, it can also be enormously freeing as school is often one of the only aspects of children's lives that remain the same when someone close to them dies. It also offers access to a range of other activities and relationships at a time when so much else is painful and unpredictable.

Moreover, when parents' own grief means that they are unable to engage with the experience of the child, teachers can play a key role in helping children make sense of their loss, express how they feel and integrate the experience into their lives (Altschuler et al., 1999; Rowling, 2010). For example, teachers may meet or speak on the telephone with the parents (or other care takers) and set up an arrangement whereby the child knows that there is a place and/or person they can go to during the day (or after school) if they feel particularly low. Because many families do not want school involved in private affairs, the school is often only asked to become involved when there is a crisis.

However, although some teachers are comfortable about speaking about bereavement, others are afraid of breaking down in front of the class. Moreover, what is rarely recognized is that the level of closeness teachers can develop with pupils means that they find themselves grieving for a loss the child is facing. With this in mind, it is important to ensure that teachers are (and feel) adequately trained. It is also important to recognize that illness and death are an integral aspect of life, find ways of discussing death as part of the usual curriculum, develop an agreed policy on how to respond when there is a death in the family, and set up structures to support teachers at such times. This includes creating a space in which it is possible for them to reflect on how to balance their roles as educators with the need to respond to the emotional needs of the child in question and the rest of the class, protect the child in question from the curiosity of others, as well as the more personal concerns discussions about death pose for them (Clay et al., 2004).

Spirituality

Throughout human history, spiritual beliefs and practices have played a significant role in anchoring and sustaining individuals, families and communities at times of loss and uncertainty (Imber-Black, 2004; Walsh, 2004). Nowhere are these beliefs and practices more important than when we are faced with our own death or the death of someone we love.

Many people draw on institutional religious beliefs and practices in order to mark the loss of a member of the family, affirm the life of the deceased, re-establish some sense of continuity and make sense of their experience. Some find strength and solace from a less traditional and more personal sense of spirituality. However, others see the notion of spirituality and faith as less relevant to them, and/or lose whatever faith they do have in the context of death.

Nonetheless, since a sizeable proportion of people look to some form of spirituality when faced with life-limiting illness and the prospect of death, it is surprising how little attention the clinical literature and trainings pay to the spiritual dimensions of illness and death (Greeff and Joubert, 2007; Peres et al., 2007). This need not mean that people do not have spiritual concerns or that those who are dying and their relatives would prefer to discuss these concerns with someone who is qualified in pastoral care. It is more likely to mean that they do not think it appropriate to discuss spirituality in clinical contexts or that health care professionals may not be open to discuss spirituality and crises of faith.

As such, it may be up to us to invite people to reflect on this aspect of their lives and its connections with the deceased (Lintz et al., 1998). This is likely to be particularly important when the deceased embodied the spiritual and/or religious beliefs of the family. This could include exploring whether or not the person or people identify with any one religious grouping, the beliefs associated with suffering and notions of personal responsibility, and differences in religious beliefs within the family. Where religion or other forms of spirituality have been an important part of their lives, it could also include exploring whether it has been possible to draw on these beliefs in coming to terms with death and, where this has been difficult, whether they would prefer to discuss this with us or a religious or spiritual leader whom they would trust.

Spirituality is often central to the way in which children and adolescents come to terms with death. For example, even if children are too young to comprehend what death means, many pray for critically ill parents, siblings, grandparents and pets and draw solace from a belief in an afterlife, for example from the belief that those who die go to heaven and are cared for by the angels. Adolescents often become more engaged with religious beliefs of their families as they grow older. This is not always the case: others tend to become less involved on leaving home (particularly where the religion of home felt oppressive) or look to forms of spirituality.

As with adults, childhood and adolescent experiences of serious illness and death can result in a crisis of faith (Roehlkepartian et al., 2006). Because our deepest convictions are shaped through the early relationships we have with parents and other care takers, one person's crisis of faith can have far-ranging implications for relationships with the rest of the family (Walsh, 2004).

In ending, I wish to emphasize that regardless of the person's age or the setting in which we work, engaging with the grief of someone else tends to confront us with our own sense of mortality. As such, it is important to pay attention to the overlaps and differences between the people with whom we work and ourselves, and guard against our own blind spots influencing what is safe to say.

Summary

- Families face four main tasks at times of bereavement: coming to some shared understanding of the reality of death; sharing aspects of their experience of loss with one another; re-organizing the family system and reworking past patterns of relating; and reinvesting in other relationships and pursuits.
- When a decision is taken to move to palliative care, it is important to treat the dying person with respect, and ensure that they are not exposed to avoidable suffering and that the care they and their relatives receive is well co-ordinated.
- Probably the most valuable input we can offer at times of death is listening and bearing witness to the distress, pain and confusion people face.
- Where people are struggling, it is also important to introduce comments and questions that open up the possibility of mourning and moving on with their lives.
- When working with children who are grieving, this includes creating opportunities in which it is possible for them to make sense of their experiences of death through play.
- Schools can play a significant role in helping children come to terms with death.
- Because many people draw strength from spirituality at times of difficulty, it can be helpful to offer them a chance to explore this aspect of their lives.

9

MIGRATION, CULTURE AND EXPERIENCES OF DIVERSITY

Migration is not a new phenomenon. However, because it has been growing at an unprecedented rate over the past three decades, far more families face the prospect of illness and death when living a considerable distance from one another. Since many health care professionals, including myself, are migrants as well, there may be times when we find ourselves offering others care we are unable to offer our own family, other than on a short-term basis. In some cases, cultural differences mean that the paradigms of illness and methods of treatment are very different from 'back home', language difficulties interfere with the possibility of reaching informed decisions about care, and where migrants are identified with groupings regarded as 'other' in the country in which they now live, they may be exposed to prejudice.

In view of the proportion of people concerned, relatively little attention has been paid to the challenges migration, cultural difference and potential exposure to prejudice pose to the recipients of health care. With important exceptions, even less attention has been paid to the impact these experiences have on health care professionals. However, the proportion of people, particularly women, from ethnic minority groups who work in the more vulnerable and less highly paid sectors of the health care services suggest that ethnic, racialized, or gendered inequalities have considerable impact on the providers as well as recipients of health care (Gulland, 2001; Henry, 2006).

Migration

Experiences of migration vary considerably. In some cases, it heralds years of isolation, economic uncertainty and exposure to prejudice. In others it allows migrants access to greater physical, economic and political security than would have been possible at home and/or an opportunity to establish a more comfortable distance in relation to their family of origin (Falicov, 1998). Similarly, while some people tend to underplay the difficulties they face, possibly as a way of dealing with the pain and guilt of parting, for others life remains dominated by loss and the image of 'what might have been' if they had lived closer to one another. However, even if the experience has been more positive, all migrations involve a level of loss and disarray. Therefore, subsequent losses, including illness, may re-evoke feelings that relate to the losses experienced as a consequence of migration.

When a migrant becomes ill

When families migrate 'en masse', providing the relationship is supportive enough, they are able to look to one another for support when ill. However, where people migrate on their own, other than on a short-term basis, families are forced to come to terms with illness and the threat of death without the practical and emotional support that would have been possible if migration had not taken place.

The absence of other close family tends to increase parents' investment in the next generation, in the 'tokens' of life in a new country. This means that at times of difficulty, they tend to turn to their children for the sort of support they might have received from the rest of the family (Koplow and Messenger, 1990).

Being there for one's parents can create a special sense of intimacy and a chance of experiencing agency when many other aspects of life feel beyond control. However, if the expectations are unmanageable, acting as parents' main source of support can disrupt traditional generational boundaries, interfering with parents' ability to discipline and children's ability to look to parents for help in making sense of their own struggles. This is particularly important to bear in mind when children act as their parents' interpreters.

Family memories offer migrants and their non-migrant kin a way of maintaining some continuity between the past and present when so much else in life is likely to have changed (Chamberlain and Leydesdorff, 2004). This is more problematic when memories of family are extremely troubled and bound up with prejudice, oppression and trauma, and cultural traditions are at odds with, or are seen to be inferior to, the traditions of the country of settlement (Altschuler, 2008). In these situations, migrants may try to disown or hide memories and traditions associated with back home to ensure that these aspects of the past do not 'contaminate' children's opportunities in this new country. However, as with all situations of censoring, the unsaid tends to break through in the nuances of what we do and say: this means the children are faced with making sense of the mismatch between what they are told and the hesitancies and gaps in what is said.

One of the other difficulties is that censoring one's past can create an artificiality that distances children from the very people who are most able to help them make sense of distressing experiences: their parents. Moreover, because most of us seek solace from memories, beliefs and practices that are familiar at times of heightened insecurity, migrants may find themselves turning to aspects of their lives they had tried to disown or censor before, for example by re-engaging with traditional practices. However, because their children and, in some cases, partners have had very little understanding of what this entails, this can give rise to tensions that are difficult to understand.

In other cases, instead of turning to their children, parents turn to one another to make up for the absence of those who are not there. As discussed in relation to children, this can create a sense of intimacy. However, it can force partners into a closeness that feels intolerable to one or both parties.

Where the person who is ill is a parent of relatively young children, non-migrant kin are sometimes able to take time out of their usual lives to help their adult child or sibling care for their children while they are less able to do so. However, despite the best intentions of both parties, this can be complicated. Although many young children find it difficult to be left in the care of anyone else when there are clearly worries within the family, this is more likely when they are left with people with whom they have only had intermittent contact, as is usually the case with grandparents, aunts or uncles who live elsewhere. Moreover, these carers will be less familiar with the children's daily routines or what they find helpful when distressed.

An added complication is that reunions tend to be seen as an opportunity to make up for gaps in contact and affirm that, despite living apart, migrant and non-migrant kin remain important to one another and are engaged with one another's lives. However, because illness-related reunions take place with the anticipation of parting once more and, where the condition is life threatening, the possibility of more permanent parting, they are also reminders of how much has changed. Moreover, even if one of the reasons for migrating was to create a more comfortable distance from the family of origin, illness and the possibility of death can trigger a longing for the closeness that felt stifling before.

In addition, the urgency of the situation tends to lead to a censoring of issues that are seen to be too difficult to resolve within the limited time they have with one another, interfering with the possibility of re-establishing a sense of connection and/or resulting in blow-ups that are confusing for all parties (Alvarez, 1999). However, this is not necessarily true: heightened awareness of how little time there is to be together can increase migrants' and non-migrants' willingness to put past differences aside.

The challenges are somewhat different in later life. Migrants' longing for the people and country they left often become more pronounced as they become older. However, going 'back home' is less feasible when they or their partner are in need of additional care: having lived else-where for so long, they are unlikely to be able to draw on a supportive network in their country of origin, and family and friends of their age may be frail or ill too, or have died (van der Geest et al., 2004). Moreover, returning is likely to mean living apart from their children at a time when they are increasingly in need of support.

Where migrants are wealthy enough, some move between their countries of settlement and origin when they retire. This enables them to maintain links with their non-migrant kin and country of origin, and where migrating involved a significant change in climate, avoid weather they find particularly challenging. However, here too moving is less feasible when one or both partners become ill.

If finances allow, some elderly non-migrant parents move to live closer to their children. This enables children to fulfil their parents' and their own expectations of filial obligation as parents become increas-ingly frail. However, moving at this stage of life means that it is more difficult to establish a new social network. As such, parents tend to be more reliant on their children than would have been the case if their children had not left or they had moved earlier, giving rise to tensions that can be difficult for both parties.

Illness and those who are 'left behind'

Within the wider psychological literature, far more attention has been paid to the challenges migrants face than to the positions of the parents, sisters and brothers who chose, or felt forced, to remain when their child or sibling left. Because much of what has been written about migration has evolved from the work of people with a personal history of migra-tion, this neglect is likely to reflect a preoccupation with their own posi-tion and/or unwillingness to confront the impact their migration has had on the lives of their non-migrant kin. This is reflected in the absence of any agreed term to denote this position. The more usual way is by prefacing 'migrant', 'immigrant' or 'emigrant' with 'non-' or using 'left behind'. However, each of these terms frames this position negatively and in relation to an experience of someone else rather than the person in question (Falicov, 1998).

In many cases, migration involves the movement of an adult child to seek better employment opportunities (Giles and Mu, 2005). If, as is often the case, parents supported their children's decision and the move signifies the fulfilment of their own dreams, they may try to hide what is troubling, including health concerns, and minimize their struggles, to avoid driving their children away by appearing to be too needy, and/or facing their increased frailty (Coles, 2001; Militiades, 2002; van der Geest et al., 2004). This makes it more difficult for migrant children to understand what parents need and help them plan for the future. This is even more difficult when experiences of illness become conflated with non-migrants' resentment and sadness about being 'left behind' and migrants' guilt, ambivalence or even relief about their decision to leave.

Here too, depending on finances and the practicalities of taking time out from other aspects of their life, adult children may be able to go back to support their non-migrant kin when there are medical crises, as tends to occur more frequently in later life. Although this enables them to provide emotional and practical support, communicate with the medical professionals and if need be recruit additional paid care, they are rarely able to do so on a long-term basis. Moreover, these times spent together and the support of paid carers cannot make up for the loneliness of being unable to turn to one's family in a more ordinary and ongoing way. This means that parents and children have to find a way of reworking their understanding and expectations of what family relationships entail in this situation and avoid frustrations about 'what might have been' dominating experience of the present as well as the past (Coles, 2001; Militiades, 2002).

Where one or more siblings have not left the country, they tend to assume more responsibility for parents and other vulnerable relatives than is true of their migrant brothers and sisters. This can work extremely well with migrant siblings supporting them and their parents with phone calls, emails, letters, and where finances permit, paying for aspects of their care and taking time out from their day-to-day lives to provide their siblings with some respite. When the relationship between non-migrant siblings and their ill parents is more problematic than is true of the relationship with migrant siblings, the experience of caring for and being cared for can result in establishing a more comfortable relationship with one another than would have been possible had their siblings remained.

Nonetheless, regardless of how comfortable siblings are with one another, because long-term care giving can be extremely burdensome, tensions can arise. Where the relationship between siblings is more fraught, differences in care-giving roles and differences that relate to the real and imagined consequences of migration may become blurred, re-evoking feelings that relate to earlier negotiations of differences. As such, it may be impossible to come to any agreement about their parents' care without addressing these earlier dynamics. This is not always the case: discussions about parents' care offer siblings who have become distant from one another an opportunity to establish greater contact.

Where difficulties arise it is sometimes possible to see migrant and non-migrant siblings together (with or without their parents). Where parents are seen as holding the family together and represent migrants' relationship to the country, one of the more painful questions underlying these differences may be whether their death will result in having less contact with one another in the future. Even if it is not possible to see the whole family together, it can be helpful to explore what they need to know, ask or share to develop a better understanding of one another's lives. This includes encouraging people to imagine how they might feel if they were in the others' place, what they might want to say to one another, how to speak in such a way that their comments could be heard rather than being experienced as criticism, what needs to happen before they are able to ask for more support and respect one another's requests.

Before moving on, in drawing attention to the challenges discussed above, my intention has not been to suggest that migration has a necessarily problematic effect on experiences of illness. Instead, it has been to show that tensions that appear to be signs of pathology and personal failure may be an almost inevitable consequence of migration.

Language and the use of interpreters

Since language is integral our ability to structure and provide meaning to experiences, form relationships and express what we need, it is hardly surprising that there appears to be a link between language proficiency, health status, use of health services and the outcome of health care (Granger and Baker, 2002; Scheppers et al., 2006). Where the recipients and providers of health care are unable to communicate in the same language, ill people and their families are less able to make sense of what the doctor, nurse or physiotherapist says, ask questions and reach informed decisions about their care. It is also more difficult for professionals to take a clear history, assess the severity of their symptoms and understand the needs of the ill person.

For example, a Dutch study found that a high percentage of GPs and home care nurses felt that problems in communicating meant that Turkish and Moroccan migrants who died had not received sufficient care, and did not have a good enough understanding of their disease, that informal carers had been unnecessarily overburdened, and there had been more difficulties in making appointments (de Graaff and Francke, 2009). Similar findings have been found in relation to the experiences of non-English-speaking hospice patients and families in English-speaking countries (McGrath et al., 2001).

In situations like this it can be extremely helpful if it is possible to be seen by a doctor, nurse or counsellor who can speak one's 'mother tongue'. However, as this is rarely feasible, in such cases it is important to:

- Draw on the services of a trained interpreter to minimize problems with accuracy, medical terminology and confidentiality (rather than children and people in the waiting room).
- Establish whether the interpreter is acceptable to the patient.
- Use the same interpreter as much as possible.
- Ensure that the patient, family, interpreter and health professional are positioned so that it is possible to maintain eye contact and notice non-verbal cues.
- Maintain eye contact with the patient and family rather than the interpreter.
- Use visual aids like drawings and gesture where needed.
- Repeat key issues and verify people's understanding.
- Where there is a marked difference in the length of what is said and translated, ask the interpreter to repeat what was said, and if necessary, return at a later point to issues that seem to be censored.

The experience of working through an interpreter can be frustrating because it is more difficult to know what has been said. It also slows the process down. However, this allows both parties a time to reflect on what has been said or asked. Although translating sentence by sentence rather than 'paragraphs' allows for greater accuracy, it halts the flow of communications. As such, it can be helpful to work with the same interpreter over a longer period of time as this allows us to reach some decisions about the pattern of interpreting. Because speaking on behalf of someone who is seriously ill is likely to confront interpreters with their own mortality (and, in some cases, memories of their own migration), it can also be helpful to allow time to debrief after ending (Granger and Baker, 2002). Debriefing sessions also offer a chance to discuss areas in which misunderstandings arise and familiarize ourselves with issues that are seen as culturally inappropriate to discuss.

However, concerns about confidentiality mean that some people prefer to ask someone from their family or friendship circle to act as their translator, particularly when they migrated from a highly politicized country, when past experiences or current living conditions are seen as shameful, and/or there is a desire to hide aspects of their lives from the immigration authorities. Because children tend to learn a new language more easily than their parents, they are sometimes expected to act as their parents' translators. This means that children may be exposed to concerns their parents would otherwise have wanted to shield them from. It can be difficult to find a word that gives an accurate sense of what we mean regardless of our age. However, the risks of inaccuracies and misunderstandings developing are higher with a child because they are likely to be required to interpret and explain issues they are too young to understand. Although this experience may fit with families' ideas of what family care means and need not prove problematic, it has the potential to disrupt intergenerational patterns of power and responsibilities. With this in mind, it can be helpful to explore what this means for families, for example whether parents are able to hold on to their sense of authority, and the impact this has on children's engagement with age-appropriate activities, particularly schooling.

In some cases, children find it more difficult than their parents to learn a new language. Because language difficulties may reflect wider problems with learning, it is important to explore this further and if necessary refer them on to a remedial or speech therapist. However, whatever one's age, difficulties in learning a new language may be indicative of a wider difficulty in embracing life in a new country. As such, it can also be helpful to offer people a space to reflect more widely on the effect migration has on their lives and the lives of their non-migrant kin.

Some parents prefer to translate for their children: indeed it may feel like one of the few ways in which they are able to care for their children when so much else is beyond their control. However, as reflected in the following example, it can be difficult to know what children understand, what they have really been told and what they might want to say if they were able to express their wants and needs themselves.

Fourteen-year-old Rani and her father Imran were referred for additional psycho-social support, shortly after she was admitted to hospital in end-stage renal failure. Rani had been diagnosed with end-stage renal failure relatively recently. As her condition was deteriorating and her father had been working in Britain for some time, her parents decided she should join him because they felt that she would receive better care here.

I was asked to see them because the medical team felt Rani was extremely withdrawn, possibly depressed, and thought the relationship with her father was particularly strained. However, they were unsure whether patterns of interacting they saw as problematic were reflective of a different cultural appreciation of father–daughter relationships.

Because Rani was unable to speak English, she was offered access to a trained interpreter but her father refused to allow anyone else to translate for his daughter as his English was fluent. However, differences in the length of what was said and translated suggested he was censoring questions and explanations he did not want her to hear. Over time, difficulties in taking time off work, and the establishment of greater trust, meant that he allowed an interpreter to translate for her when he could not be there. Having been largely silent before, Rani was more open in voicing her own concerns, including worries about her health and how much she was missing her mother, younger siblings and friends.

When the interpreter cancelled at short notice, I suggested we go ahead with the meeting because I suspected that Rani understood more than she acknowledged. During this session, we communicated by using gesture, facial expressions and a few English words. Where Rani seemed to find it particularly difficult to express herself I suggested she use her own language and tried to learn words that appeared to carry particular meaning. The lack of a shared language meant there was a great deal we could not say or understand. Indeed, it is worth noting that where migrants' earlier experiences have been particularly traumatic, it is sometimes easier to share this in a language that is less familiar before being able to process emotionally laden thoughts, feelings and fantasies in one's own (Burck, 2005).

However, in this context, my guess is that both of us had to dig deeper and possibly drew on aspects of ourselves we might otherwise underplay in such situations. It is therefore probably not surprising that Rani used this session to voice issues she had not raised in front of her father or interpreter, including uncertainty about the cause of renal failure and her long-term prognosis, and discomfort with the amount of attention that was being paid to her body. This helped me realize that because Rani had been so ill when first admitted, I, the rest of the team and her father had underplayed the fact that she had been faced with coming to terms with the deterioration in her health and having to commence a strict regime of treatment at the same time as moving to a country in which she did not understand the language. Moreover, because her mother was not able to join her until much later, instead of being able to turn to the person who had been her main source of support, she was only able to turn to a father whom she had seen on a fairly intermittent basis before, who was likely to see the care of children as the responsibility of a mother and wary of jeopardising his wife's chances of being granted permission to enter the country to care for Rani.

Cultural diversity and exposure to prejudice

Over the past thirty years, there has been a growth in research and initiatives aimed at promoting greater cultural sensitivity, respect for the religious and cultural beliefs of all recipients of health care, attending to differences in access to resources and fostering an environment in which diversity is not only acknowledged but welcomed and seen as beneficial (Coker, 2001; Department of Health, 2010).

Unfortunately, translating the aims discussed above into action has fallen behind what had been hoped. This probably relates to such factors as unclear goals, a lack of appropriate knowledge and methods of training, and ambiguities about what terms like 'culture' and 'ethnicity' actually mean. For example, 'ethnicity' tends to be used to refer to a sense of belonging and acceptance of the group mores and practices of a particular culture. However, terms like 'Asian', 'Jewish' or 'Pakistani' are over-simplistic: they ignore the fact that ethnicities shift in response to altered circumstances, rates of assimilation and/or acculturation (Hillier and Kelleher, 1996; Phoenix and Pattyama, 2006). Nonetheless, ethnicity appears to inform doctors' patterns of referral regardless of the severity of the condition (Karim et al., 2000).

Similarly, although asking health care users to fill in forms marked with 'White British', 'Black British', 'Asian' or 'Other' might be aimed at ensuring all sectors of the population have equal access to health care, these terms are a conflation of racialized and ethnic categories. Moreover, relying on these categories fails to take account of concerns about the way in which this sort of data can be and has been abused, as in apartheid-based South Africa, Nazi Germany and Rwanda.

Attempts to enshrine greater respect for all groupings also needs to take account of the fact that no culture is static and ideas about health care and family life change in relation to altered circumstances. For example, Chinese cultures are generally assumed to be more accepting of illness than in the west, view dementia as an expected part of aging and see the responsibility of caring for vulnerable relatives as lying with members of their family. However, factors like increased longevity, rising numbers of people with degenerative and disabling conditions, and shorter hospital stays mean that, in common with other families, Chinese families are finding this increasingly difficult and are therefore less willing to assume primary responsibility of caring for the vulnerable and the old, as was the case before.

It is important to take account of the more irrational feelings about foreigners and people who are seen to be different. As discussed earlier, one way of dealing with situations that are evoked by loss and uncertainty is to project what is hated and feared onto others, particularly those deemed to be outsiders. This is more likely when the people concerned are migrants and/or are identified with groupings deemed to be 'other', and when the condition they have is seen to relate to their position as a foreigner, as is the case in relation to tuberculosis (TB) and to some extent HIV/AIDs in many first world contexts (Craig, 2007; Joffe, 2007).

It is also important to recognize that differences in constructions of health care can lead to misunderstandings neither party is aware of. For example, although western cultures tend to place a high value on a sense of autonomy and intimacy with a partner, many eastern and African cultures place a higher value on interdependence and relationships with another person from one's family, peer or friendship circle (Kleinman et al., 2006; Krause, 1998). This means that practices informed by an individual's right to make decisions about their care may be antithetical to people from cultures which prioritize life over a more comfortable death and place a higher value on experiences of connectedness than individuality. In addition, communicating in more indirect ways than is usual in the west may not be withholding, but indicative of a different appreciation of, what is appropriate when someone is ill and facing the possibility of death (Tse et al., 2003).

Even when these differences are less pronounced, there are likely to be times when migrants are reminded of their position as an outsider. For example, American-born Charlotte found that although the questions she asked the medical team were based on a patient's legitimate right to information, because her style was more forthright than is usual in Britain, they were experienced as rude and aggressive. Similarly, although she appreciated the fact that living in Britain entitled her to free health care, she resented the lack of choice this entailed and felt her chances of survival would have been higher had she been treated in the United States.

Where these differences are more obvious, people whose responses are different from those that are regarded as usual in the country in which they live have an increased risk of being labelled as abnormal, and their symptoms of being treated with suspicion. Drawing on her own work as a GP, Hopkins (2002) suggests that some of this suspicion may be a way of dealing with the powerlessness GPs experience when the symptoms (for example, experiences of pain) people present do not accord with what one has learnt, and language barriers mean that it is more difficult to understand what is needed, resulting in becoming oppositional and labelling what is not understood as imaginary or 'psychosomatic'.

Anthropological research suggests that there is an increased tendency to somatize psychological distress when people are from cultures (or families) where acknowledging psychological distress is seen to bring shame on the family (Krause, 1998). However, it is important to respect the fact that these symptoms are real, even if they reflect a combination of psychological and physical distress. This is particularly important to bear in mind when people are refugees, have fled under difficult circumstances, and their status in the country is unclear (Jones and Paramjit, 1998). It is worth noting that where people are particularly isolated, GPs and the rest of the health care team may stand 'in loco' for the extended family: even if difficulties in understanding what is wrong (including language difficulties) mean that consultations do not always meet the needs of the patient, they offer people a chance of feeling they are taken care of and respected.

Reflecting on his work with people who rely on non-western methods of treatment, Flores (2000) argues similarly that instead of becoming oppositional it is more helpful to encourage people to draw on both forms of treatment. This is partly because non-western treatments might prove helpful, and if they do not, need not cause harm, and partly because it reduces the likelihood of a delay in relying more wholeheartedly on western medicine should other methods fail.

Analysis of the experiences of people with sickle cell anaemia (particularly experiences of pain control) suggests that the risk of one's symptoms being treated with suspicion is particularly high when the condition one suffers from is more prevalent amongst certain ethnic and racialized groups (Dyson et al., 2006). One way of ensuring that all sectors of the population receive appropriate care is to try to ensure that they are seen by a health professional with a similar background (Anionwu, 1996). However, this is rarely feasible and has the potential to frame this aspect of identity as more important than all others, positioning both parties as 'other'.

Another option is to ask people about their beliefs, experiences and expectations of health care. Although this means we are more aware of issues they see as particularly important, they are unlikely to know where our gaps in understanding lie. In addition, this may be experienced as emphasizing their sense of foreignness and not belonging. It is also unfair to burden people who are seriously ill with the task of acting as 'cultural interpreters'. Other possibilities include drawing on the literature and consulting with colleagues who identify with that group. However, it is important to respect the fact that the views of one person, even if they are an academic or health care professional, are never able to capture the views or experience of an entire cultural group. As such, it is important to tread carefully to avoid attempts to understand others' practices and beliefs being experienced as disrespectful.

For example, Chang, a Chinese man, and Emily, a white British woman, asked for help in explaining to their children that their father was dying. The work ended after meeting with them and their young children for a limited period of time. I was re-contacted by Emily a few months after he died because she was finding it difficult to help her children come to terms with their father's death and was struggling to come to terms with her own sense of grief. On meeting with Emily I found that the main issue she wanted to discuss was her confusion and anger about her parents-in-law's refusal to attend Chang's funeral and reluctance to engage more with their grandchildren. My reading of the literature suggested that although Chinese people tend to be more accepting of illness and death than in the west, this is not true when a child (and in this case an only child) dies, because children are required to perform certain rituals at their parents' funeral. As such, a child's death poses a threat to the wellbeing of their surviving parents and of the wider community.

Exploring how cultural difference might be affecting the relationship between her and her parents-in-law helped Emily think more widely about her interactions with them, leading to a discussion of whether some of the anger towards her was an expression of their disapproval of Chang's life style and choice of partner, and their inability to reach some sort of reconciliation before his death. However, as the work progressed it became apparent that underlying Emily's anger towards her parents-in-law was the anger she felt towards Chang for leaving her with two young and very needy children.

As reflected above, when working cross-culturally, it is important to listen, learn, and remain sensitive to potential areas of difference. For example, while some form of physical contact (such as shaking hands or a hug) and exchanging information about one's self and family is seen as a way of greeting and recognizing the personhood of another within certain cultures, this is not the case in others. As such, interactions that are aimed at being respectful may be experienced as cold or inappropriate. Other potential differences include:

- Embodied experiences of health and illness.
- Signs that are indicative of illness.
- Understandings of the cause of illness and expectations of treatment.
- Attitudes towards communicating pain and suffering, disclosure, truth telling and acceptable levels of physical contact.
- Aging, spirituality and the notion of an afterlife.
- Expectations of childhood.
- Gendered expectations of roles and responsibility.
- Acceptance of outside support, including doctors, nurses and psychotherapists.

In some cases, it may be important to alter the way we work, for example by going more slowly, being mindful of how we ask questions and speak as well as what is said and asked, remaining alert to the possibility of misunderstandings and aware of times when communication seems to be breaking down, and familiarizing ourselves with issues that are likely to be important. However, it is also important to avoid using cultural difference as the main way of understanding experiences of illness and death or the ways in which we respond and interact. Indeed, cross-cultural work draws attention to an issue that is central to all work with illness: the importance of being able to ask questions, make informed guesses, lay aside our assumptions and draw on our shared experience of humanity.

This does not mean turning a blind eye to practices that are illegal and situations where cultural beliefs are used to justify abusive relationships, for example the abuse of women and children. It is important to guard against blaming people who are deemed to be 'other' for practices that occur more widely as it is not amongst migrants and racialized 'others' that women are at risk of being subordinated and oppressed, and where the views and rights of children are not respected.

Summary

- Increased rates of migration mean that far more people face the prospect of illness and death when living apart from close family, many professionals are in a position of offering others care they cannot offer members of their own family, and the paradigms of treatment are very different from what they would have been back home.
- Where migration has taken place, it is possible to frame the difficulties that emerge in terms of migration even if they are quite unrelated.
- Migrants tend to look to partners and children to make up for the absence of other family members at times of crisis.
- When young adults migrate, they are rarely able to provide parents and siblings who stay 'behind' the emotional and practical support they need at times of illness.
- Since language is integral to our ability to understand experiences, form relationships and express what we need, where people are not fluent in the language of the professionals entrusted with their care it is important to offer access to the services of a trained interpreter.
- When working cross-culturally, misunderstandings can arise that neither party is aware of.
- However, this work highlights an issue that is central to all health care: the need to respect religious and cultural beliefs, foster an environment in which diversity is welcomed, and attend to differences in resources and opportunities.

10

PERSONAL–PROFESSIONAL ASPECTS OF HEALTH CARE

Caring for and helping to ease the suffering of people who are ill or dying can be enormously rewarding. However, there are many situations where, despite the best efforts of the medical team, the ill person and their family, instead of our being able to cure and ease distress, the people we are caring for die or are left severely disabled. As a result, this work has the potential to confront us with our own sense of mortality and powerlessness, giving rise to feelings that can be difficult to manage or understand.

Unaddressed and unacknowledged, exposure to ongoing stress can result in 'burn out', 'secondary traumatization' and 'compassion fatigue', which includes such responses as denying how we feel, intellectualizing, acting in self-destructive ways (taking drugs and drinking excessively), worries about personal health, intrusive dreams, and distancing ourselves from the people entrusted to our care. As such, work that starts out as meaningful becomes unfulfilling and meaningless, energy turns into exhaustion, involvement into cynicism and efficacy into ineffectiveness (Firth-Cozens, 2003).

Despite the profound effect this can have on the experiences of the people we are caring for, relatively little academic attention has been paid to more personal, non-clinical challenges this work presents, and few health care courses offer trainees sufficient preparation in dealing with these challenges. This chapter is an attempt to address this gap.

Potential sources of stress

Experiences of stress vary: while many of us find operating at fairly high levels of pressure stimulating, others find it impossible to tolerate similar levels of pressure. Moreover, situations that seem manageable at certain times are less so at others. Nonetheless, the following factors tend to inform the amount of stress to which health care professionals are exposed:

- The age of the person who is ill or dying.
- The nature of the actual condition.
- Whether or not our work corresponds with our professional role, position in the hierarchy, status and financial reward.
- The structure of the work setting.
- The extent to which we feel supported, personally and professionally.
- The fit between the values of the organization and our own.
- Personal histories of illness and other forms of loss.

For example, the untimely nature of death in a young child means that it can be particularly difficult to tell families that a child or adolescent is terminally ill. This is partly because it is difficult to know how much children can understand, what parents have told them and are prepared for them to hear. The challenges are somewhat different when they are older: like adults, adolescents tend to be more challenging of professional decisions and the care that is on offer.

As indicated above, the nature of the actual condition informs the challenges professionals face as well. For example, because jaundice, MRSA (a skin bacterium that is resistant to a range of antibiotics) and HIV/AIDs are contagious, one of the challenges professionals face when working with these conditions is ensuring they do not become infected. However, the fear and stigma associated with such conditions, particularly HIV/AIDs, mean that professionals are also likely to be faced with the discomfort of wanting to distance themselves from people who represent illness, contagion and death.

Increased access to antiviral drugs means that a higher proportion of people with the HIV virus are able to survive, provided they adhere to a strict treatment regime for the rest of their lives. As with other conditions where non-adherence can lead to a rapid deterioration in health, in these situations, professionals have to find a way of remaining supportive when the affected person seems unable or unwilling to maximize their chances of survival. However, because HIV/AIDs can be sexually transmitted, professionals are also faced with the challenge of raising complicated moral and relational questions people may be reluctant to consider, such as how and when to disclose one's status to a potential sexual partner and, in the case of parents, how to tell children that they and/or their children have been infected and prepare them for the questions their status raises for their friends (Wouters et al., 2009; PATA, 2010).

In resource-starved areas where the prevalence of HIV/AIDs is particularly high, a number of hospitals and clinics are beginning to delegate tasks that have been the responsibility of doctors to staff with lower-level qualifications. Initial reports suggest task shifting is a viable way of addressing this gap in resources (Callaghan et al., 2010). Similarly positive results have been found in relation to training 'expert patients', lay people who are HIV positive, to undertake some of the tasks that are usually carried out by professionals. However, in both cases, this is only effective when they have access to training and ongoing supervision in which it is possible to reflect on such issues as the meaning of working in an illness-related field when one does not have the appropriate professional qualification, and in the case of 'expert patients', the link between their own experience and that of the people with whom they are working.

Moreover, in contexts where the availability of antiviral drugs is limited, health care professionals spend much of their time with people who are dying. As discussed in the previous chapter, regardless of the diagnosis, watching someone die can be enormously distressing, giving rise to feelings of powerlessness, failure and shame. However, watching someone die is even more distressing when one feels that her or his death could have been prevented (Mathers and Gask, 1995).

Shifts in practice and policy

Advances in medical knowledge and technology have had an enormously positive impact on health care. Developments in technology mean that it is more possible to keep people alive on life support machines than before. The internet and website blogs mean that people who are too ill to go out are more able to be in contact with friends and people who have the same condition, and mobile phone messaging is proving to be an effective way of increasing adherence and attendances at medical appointments (Lester et al., 2010).

However, in many cases, these advances mean that professionals are responsible for tasks that were not addressed in our original training. For example, instead of offering the sort of care that had drawn nurses to this area of work, they often find themselves caught up with monitoring equipment that breaks down and leads to false alarms.

Moreover, although initiatives aimed at saving costs, streamlining resources and the closer monitoring of services are likely to prove beneficial, they tend to increase professionals' administrative load and require a reworking of clinical practice. Where cost cutting relates to essential services, nurses as well as many other professionals work over-time on an ongoing basis to avoid lowering standards of care. Furthermore, although the decision to shorten hospital admissions has meant ill people are parted from their families for shorter periods of time, those who are admitted tend to be more ill and require more specialized treatment than before. As a result, professionals are likely to be working with people who are too ill to communicate, may not survive and have less opportunity to develop a relationship with them, an aspect of care that tends to be sustaining to both parties. This shift in practice also means that a greater proportion of professionals (particularly nurses) work in the community, where they are not only less protected and more isolated than before, but are working with people who are themselves extremely isolated (Wilkinson, 1995).

Other significant shifts include increased engagement with the recip-ients of health care and encouraging (or allowing) recipients to take more responsibility for managing their own care. Both initiatives are proving to be an effective way of improving providers' understanding of what the recipients of the service need and want and of combating the sense of powerlessness and dependency that tends to set in when ill. However, they have also meant that professionals have had to learn new skills, such as how to encourage people to assume greater responsibility for their health, and tend to be faced with people who are challenging of the care they receive.

Ambiguities in roles and responsibilities

It tends to be less stressful where it is clear where one's role and respon-sibilities start and end. However, in medical settings, the boundaries between roles and areas of responsibility are often blurred, particularly in settings where holistic care is important, as in palliative care. As such, tensions that appear to reflect personality clashes may be an expression of confusion about roles and areas of responsibility (Firth, 2003).

It also tends to be less stressful when the work we are required to do corresponds with positions in the hierarchy, status and salary. However, this is often not the case: although senior doctors carry ultimate respon-sibility for questions of care, providing the main input on issues like prognosis and helping people assimilate what this means, in many situ-ations these tasks fall to more junior doctors and nurses, to staff less able to 'escape' the questions the ill person and their family pose (Escot et al., 2001).

When the condition is long term, one of the challenges profession-als face is that families may know far more about the condition and advances in care than the professionals, particularly newcomers to this work. Professionals also have to find a way of making sense of the famil-iarity that tends to develop when interacting with ill people and their families over a long period. In her analysis of interactions between fami-lies, nurses and doctors caring for children in a transitional care unit, Down (2010) found that nurses and families described these relation-ships as personal and akin to friendship while doctors described them as professional and task-oriented. This suggests that interactions that are intended to be supportive can be experienced as inappropriate or unsupportive.

In contrast, in situations in which the family contributes more actively to medical care, as in giving a child an injection or managing home dialysis, if problems occur, professionals have to find a way of remaining positive and help the family deal with their disappointment and frustration without getting caught up with blame, even if they suspect the problems were the result of the family's mismanagement or because the instructions they had given the family were unclear.

Maintaining 'professional' boundaries

Most health care trainings are based on the idea that it is not only preferable but also possible to maintain a clear boundary between ourselves and the people entrusted to our care. However, whilst there is some agreement about the need to avoid forms of self-disclosure, touch and expressions of concern that could be misinterpreted, there is less agreement about what maintaining this boundary actually means in practice (Brennan and Moynihan, 2004).

It is obviously important to maintain some boundary to avoid personal identifications interfering with the work we are required to do. However, maintaining a more distant approach appears to have a disempowering effect on ill people, increasing the likelihood of non-adherence, ineffective use of resources, over-utilization of medical serves, 'doctor shopping' and litigation claims (Coyle, 1999; Gandhi et al., 1997). Moreover, denying that we are moved by people's experience is often not only impossible but enormously exhausting: as such, it tends to increase rather than decrease the stress associated with this work (Balint, 1993).

Furthermore, as exposure to people who are ill and dying tends to confront us with our own sense of mortality and limitations, the emphasis placed on maintaining 'appropriate boundaries' may be an attempt to protect professionals from people who evoke these feelings. It may also be a way to avoid facing the fact that in many cases, although it is widely accepted that it is inappropriate to look at the body of some-one with whom one is not intimate, or to cause pain or distress, professionals are required to do so. For example, surgeons are generally seen to act in a more detached way than other professionals. This is likely to relate to a concern to safeguard clinical judgement and accuracy. However, because their work is invasive, potentially life-threatening but in some cases involves operating on someone who is not in obvious discomfort, it is also likely to relate to a desire to avoid identifying with the potentially mutilating nature of the work they are required to do.

The potential to identify with the damaging or invasive nature of the work we do is relevant to the work of other professionals as well: although chemo- and radiotherapy might increase the chances of survival, in the short term both forms of treatment tend to make people feel more unwell. Similarly, where people are unable to deal with the challenges they face, as counsellors and psychotherapists we may feel it would be helpful for them to reflect on aspects of their lives they seem reluctant to face. However, this can feel inappropriate when they are contending with many other invasions of their physical and emotional privacy.

Disentangling the personal and professional

Unconscious phenomena mean we can never be fully aware of the ways in which our own thoughts and feelings inform interactions with others. However, as these thoughts and feelings can have a profound effect on the ways in which we relate to others, it is important to increase our awareness of what psychoanalysts call 'transference' and 'counter-transference' phenomena.

'Transference' refers to situations where our thoughts and responses seem to be a reflection of issues that relate more to the people with whom we work than to ourselves. Reflecting on the possibility of a link can alert us to concerns that people are unable or reluctant to raise. It can also alert us to situations where tensions between the staff might be a reflection of tensions that relate to the family they are working with. Transference is likely to account for why asking medical students to present case studies (in this study, people with HIV/AIDs) as if they were discussing their life tends to increase their investment in the outcome of treatment and patients' future (Marshall and O'Keefe, 1995).

In contrast, 'counter-transference' refers to situations where the views we have about others are less about their experience than our own. As such, reflecting on the links with our own experiences can alert us to the ways in which blind spots limit our ability to engage with the suffering of others and/or times when the stress we experience relates not to external demands but to our own unattainable goals. This is particularly important because work with illness and death tends to face us with loss at so many levels, including the losses evoked by:

- Identifying with someone who is seriously ill and may die.
- Being unable to reach one's professional goals, as when someone dies or is discharged before all treatment possibilities are exhausted.
- Challenges to our assumptions of how life should be.
- The death of someone we have come to know well over the course of their illness.[1]

For example, I was asked to see 6-year-old Tony and his mother Felicia, a woman who had been diagnosed with a severe form of breast cancer, because he had become increasingly aggressive at school. When I met the family, Felicia began a long account of her difficulties, of how her parents had migrated leaving her in the care of an unsupportive grandmother when she was young, of being abandoned by Tony's father before he was born, and her recent diagnosis of breast cancer. Whenever I tried to slow the pace and build on Tony's attempts to distract his mother, Felicia returned to her own story. Moreover, despite speaking openly in front of him, she said he did not know she had cancer and she did not want to discuss this with him.

As the session continued I felt increasingly powerless, irritated and unable to concentrate. I became so distracted that when Tony scratched a deep hole in his drawing and his mother said 'Silly – I don't have a hole there' I was unable to make the link with what his mother had been saying. It was only when a colleague working with me (Barbara Dale) drew my attention to this that I was able to re-engage and ask Felicia what she thought her son had been trying to tell her.

Imagining myself in her position helped me see that I had been made to feel some of what Felicia was experiencing: I felt swamped by uncontained and uncontainable information, distressed by the fact that Tony was likely to lose his mother at such a young age and embarrassed by what I saw as Felicia's insensitivity to her son and my inability to protect him from what seemed like an assault. It also helped me recognize that my struggle to hold on to a sense of professional competence might mirror Felicia and Tony's attempts to control the uncontrollable, how lonely and exhausted she might feel, how hard it might be to share her fears with others, particularly fears about the effect being ill might have on her son. However, it also put me in touch with some of the more personal issues her situation triggered for me: although there were many differences between Felicia and me, including differences in health status, experiences of childhood, educational and professional opportunities, like her I have been through times when my own preoccupations have affected my ability to recognize the concerns of my own children.

One way of increasing our understanding of these links is to recall an illness event or another situation of adversity that took place when we were younger and try to remember:

- The beliefs we and our family had drawn on.
- How issues of blame, shame and guilt were dealt with.
- How this experience affects our current beliefs, including beliefs about the value of being optimistic or realistic in the face of adversity and the role families should play.
- How these experiences have affected responses to subsequent experiences of adversity and clinical situations we find challenging.[2]

It can be helpful to construct a genogram to trace the ways in which stories of illness, loss, care and control have been transmitted across the generations, and reflect on how this relates to situations we find challenging.

It is also important to reflect on the impact of this work on relationships in the here and now. Working with illness and death tends to increase our awareness of the likelihood of illness and death, giving rise to a desire to prepare are ourselves for these eventualities, for example by making sure others have an understanding of our end-of-life plans. Because this relates to experiences our families are not part of, they may not be ready to discuss this. They may also be reluctant to listen to reminders of illness and death, particularly where this work seems to take priority over family life. However, there may be times when the opposite is true, when we distance ourselves from them to avoid confronting the feelings this work evokes in ourselves.

One issue that is more relevant to doctors and nurses is that because they are trained to treat illness, it can be difficult to know how to respond when a friend or family member has serious health concerns. As such, before responding, useful questions to consider include:

- Am I able to be objective enough to give an accurate assessment and share worrying news if need be?

- Am I adequately trained to treat this problem?
- How will acting in a professional capacity affect future family/friendship relationships?
- Would they receive better care from someone else?
- Can I allow someone else to deal with this?
- Will my family or friends understand if I stand back?[3]

On caring for the carers

As many of the stresses professionals face relate to external phenomena, it is important to find ways of minimizing these stressors or responding differently. There is a great deal managers are doing and can do to reduce the demands professionals face:

- Create a supportive atmosphere in which personal struggles can be acknowledged.
- Clarify roles and areas of responsibility.
- Offer staff opportunities to contribute to decisions.
- Ensure staff at all levels have access to supervision.
- Run trainings aimed at enhancing professionals' ability to deal with challenging situations, for example, on communication and working with families.

A number of initiatives have been introduced to reduce the stresses professionals tend to face. These include initiatives aimed at limiting the intensity of face-to-face patient contact and the responsibility any one professional carries, as in reducing the time junior doctors are required to work and arranging nurses' schedules so that they alternate between medical, surgical and emergency wards. However, any such attempts to restructure services need to take account of factors that contribute to job satisfaction as well (Menzies-Lyth, 1960). For example, these two initiatives tend to mean that there is less chance of experiencing the satisfaction that comes from caring on a more continual basis. They also mean that ill people who are facing many other forms of loss are forced to engage with a changing group of people.

Amongst the most helpful steps managers and senior clinicians can take is to encourage staff, particularly new staff, to maintain a balance between their professional and personal lives and recognize the importance of attending to their own needs. However, unless managers and senior clinicians acknowledge their own vulnerability, for example by taking off time when ill, the message they convey is that it is possible to carry on regardless of the circumstances.

The growing numbers of professionals participating in Balint groups and Schwartz Rounds attest to increased awareness of the benefits of being able to acknowledge one's vulnerabilities, reflect on the more complex emotional issues health care work presents, and discuss situations professionals feel less able and untrained to address. Informed by psychoanalytic theory, Balint groups were established with a view to increasing general practitioners' sensitivity to doctor–patient relationships, patients' reactions and the feelings and motivations that underpin their own responses. However, these groups are now attended by other health care professionals as well (Balint, 1993; Matalon and Mazor, 1999; Mathers and Gask, 1995). In contrast, inspired by Schwartz's experience of cancer, Schwartz Rounds are a multidisciplinary forum in which professionals are encouraged to discuss the psycho-social issues patients, families and other caregivers face, reflect on the concerns they have and gain insight from the experience of fellow professionals (Manning, 2010; Wolpin et al., 2005). Although there are differences between the two, attendance at both forums has been found to increase participants' ability to cope with the psychosocial demands of care (including 'heart sink cases'), provide compassionate care and, where professionals are in the same team, improve staff dynamics.

Supervision

Supervision has a critically important role to play in supporting and extending the professional development of health care professionals (Kilminster and Jolly, 2000; Launer and Halpern, 2006). Supervision has been found to be of benefit to the emotional wellbeing and clinical skills of medical as well as mental health professionals, regardless of their level of experience or the urgency of the cases under discussion (Bogo and McKnight, 2004; Kilminster and Jolly, 2000). For example, although junior doctors appear to benefit from opportunities to exercise autonomy, insufficient access to supervision is associated with increased numbers of deaths and an acceptance of lower standards of care (Sox et al., 1998).

However, to date this aspect of the work has received little research and academic attention, particularly in relation to medical professionals. This is unfortunate as the increased pressure to monitor services, media exposure of misjudgements and gaps in care, and changes in policy mean that it is even more important than before to prove that the care on offer reflects best practice.

The structure and process of supervision

Although the purpose and mode of delivery will vary depending on the tasks, roles and level of experience, in general the main aims of supervision include:

- Ensuring the safety of the patient or client.
- Offering guidance on issues pertaining to patient care.
- Enhancing professional development.
- Attending to the more personal challenges this work presents.
- Monitoring the quality of care.

Live supervision is particularly helpful when the work involves procedures and techniques that are unfamiliar: it allows the supervisor to model what is being taught and offer supervisees immediate feedback. However, there is a greater risk of supervisors taking over and deskilling the supervisee, albeit unwittingly. This is particularly problematic where prior experiences such as racism have sensitized supervisees to the likelihood that their skills will not be respected.

In contrast, retrospective supervision enables us to focus on what supervisees remember as well as their own reflections on their work. However, it relies on the accuracy of what people remember and choose to report. Nonetheless, it offers people a space to reflect on the more complicated issues their work presents. In both cases, where supervision is at the behest of management, a number of issues need to be covered at the outset:

- The aims and objectives of supervision.
- Why a decision was taken to offer supervision at this time.
- The length and frequency of sessions.
- Confidentiality.
- The relationship between supervision and assessment.
- How supervisees were selected and the optimal number to include (group supervision).
- The theoretical framework on which supervision will be based.

In my own case, this means explaining what a systemic approach entails and that the work is likely to focus on three linked themes:

- Direct clinical work.
- The dynamics of the organization.
- Personal–professional connections to the work.

Although these issues are important to cover, on meeting the supervisees it is also important to explore what they are hoping for, their past experiences of supervision, how they see their strengths and weaknesses, and to establish ground rules for this work.

Individual supervision means that it is more possible to attend to the needs of that person, allows for a deep exploration of issues that are troubling, and lessens the demands on supervisees' time. In contrast, group supervision offers a chance to reflect on and learn from the experiences of others, and where supervisees are from the same team, to make sense of the more problematic dynamics that can arise: even if people feel unable to discuss these difficulties, reflecting on clinical work together can lead to increased understanding of one another's positions.

I find it preferable to meet once a month for an hour and a half (in the case of individual supervision) or two hours (in the case of groups). Although this is not always possible, restricting the group supervision to three or four people helps to ensure that each person is able to reflect on issues they are concerned about at every session.

When people are seen individually, we usually begin by setting an agenda before focusing on the issues they would like to discuss, why a particular issue is of concern now, and how they have attempted to address their concerns. Although group supervision is similar, I tend to leave space to discuss issues of mutual concern before asking someone to begin. The supervisor and group listen to the issue they present until that person has said all they need to say (usually about ten minutes). After that the presenter is asked to remain silent while the group and I reflect on what they have said. Instead of using 'you', they are referred to in the third person. When the group contributions have ended, the person whose concerns we have been discussing is asked to reflect on what was said.

This is based on the idea that listening and reflecting on how people's comments resonate with our experience without being able to defend our own position helps to shift the stories we hold into a 'thicker' story that takes account of issues we had not thought of before (Anderson, 1987). Asking everyone to comment helps to ensure that those who are less confident are heard and that the expertise of each person is recognized, rather than framing all expertise as belonging to the supervisor. This process also means that it is possible to check whether the issues that have been raised fit with what the supervisee needs and wants from supervision.

Where supervisees are from the same professional background, reflecting on each other's stories can help in separating concerns that relate to one's professional role from concerns that are more personal. In contrast, where the group is multidisciplinary, it can increase understandings of the dilemmas other professionals face.

Two mapping exercises are useful to introduce fairly early on. The first involves mapping the participants' positions in the organization, including formal and informal roles, and constructing a time line showing significant changes in the organization and roles they are expected to play. This helps in disentangling issues that are more personal from those that relate to ambiguities in roles and areas of responsibility. Genograms are also useful to introduce early on as they present personal and professional links as integral to all health care. However, as we tend to speak more openly once greater trust has been established, both exercises form the basis for subsequent work.

Because we are more able to see alternatives and remain stimulated by our work when we adopt an observer position in relation to the issues we find challenging, it can be helpful for supervisees to select one or two issues to 'research' further. Rather than undertaking formal research, this means taking note of how these issues are addressed (or ignored) in the literature and, most importantly, how they are reflected in clinical settings.

Challenges supervisees often raise

Before outlining some of the main concerns people bring to supervision, I would like to ask you, the reader, to think about the sorts of issues you might want to raise in supervision, for example:

- What personal and professional issues you would want to explore.
- What issues colleagues, managers, friends and family would suggest you address.
- How these differ from issues you would have wanted to discuss a year ago.
- How this relates to changes in the organization or your personal life.
- Who you tend to look to in trying to make sense of these experiences.
- What would help you reflect on these concerns further.[4]

My own experience and reading of the literature suggests that, amongst the main clinical dilemmas health care professionals face, are how to deal with situations where:

- Someone is highly defensive and unwilling to acknowledge how ill they are, or someone close to them is.
- The family interfere with the ill person's ability to express their own needs, or disagree with 'do-not-resuscitate' wishes.
- There are worries about the safety of vulnerable children and adults.
- Serious mental health difficulties pre-date the onset of illness.
- There are disagreements about the boundaries of professional confidentiality (usually between medical and mental health professionals).
- There are worries about personal safety.
- Cultural and religious beliefs and language barriers interfere with communication.
- People describe and experience physical symptoms in terms that do not accord with western medicine.

Concerns about organizational issues include how to deal with situations where:

- Staff members feel they are being bullied.
- Staff dynamics are affecting patient care.
- There is a lack of trust and an escalation in tensions amongst the staff.
- Changes in policies do not fit with the ideas the staff hold dear.

Senior clinical and management staff tend to focus more on the pressure to keep up with changes in policy and cut costs without compromising care, and what to do when the quality of care is not good enough, particularly where the staff member in question is extremely vulnerable or likely to retire in a few years.

In contrast, amongst the more personal concerns to arise are how to:

- Protect the boundary between one's personal and professional life, particularly in situations of emergency that require working overtime on an ongoing basis.
- Remain alert to times when the work triggers feelings that relate to one's own experience.
- Support vulnerable colleagues when exhausted and depleted oneself.
- Deal with 'survivor guilt' and the anxieties work with people who are ill and dying raises in oneself and one's family.

For example, during individual supervision, Adam, a psychologist working in palliative care, raised a difficult personal dilemma. He was to undergo surgery that could be life-threatening. Although he wanted to avoid face-to-face contact with people who were dying, until the operation was over, he was reluctant to do so as this would mean telling his colleagues and manager about his health concerns and he was desperate to avoid being treated like a 'patient'.

Here as elsewhere, while reflexive forms of supervision allow for discussions that lie on the boundary between the personal and professional, it is important to move between these two domains. In this case, the session ended with a brief discussion of what Adam's experience had taught him about the dilemmas of the people with whom he was working. In other cases, it has been felt more appropriate to suggest people explore their concerns further in a setting that is not constrained by work.

Challenges supervisors tend to face

Factors like the contract of supervision and fit between our own clinical experience and that of the supervisees inform the sorts of challenges supervisors face. However, challenges that often arise include how to:

- Hold on to the position of a supervisor and avoid acting like a manager.
- Help staff focus on clinical work when organization difficulties feel overwhelming.
- Offer realistic feedback in a way that respects the integrity of the supervisee.
- Ensure that supervision does not veer into becoming therapy.
- Remain alert to prejudice in ourselves as well as others.

One of the more complicated issues relates to power. Where the supervisor is the person's manager or reports to management, these sessions can be used to monitor staff performance and the quality of the service. However, in these situations supervisees tend to be more wary of exposing their vulnerability and raising issues that might affect the way they are seen and their chances of promotion. Nonetheless, even when working on an external basis, there needs to be some provision for situations in which the quality of care is not good enough.

When working on a more external basis, there may be times when supervisees' accounts suggest that ambiguities in organization and gaps in management are affecting patient care and contributing to tensions amongst the staff. In trying to help people make sense of these experiences, it is important to recognize that instead of stepping into the shoes of management, our role is to encourage supervisees to reflect on their experience, explore alternative ways of addressing the dilemmas they face, and in exceptional cases, consider whether it might be helpful to share their concerns with the more senior staff. It is also important to recognize that frustration with management might relate to other sources of frustration, for example unavoidable budget cuts, and more personal sources of frustration. However, we also need to bear in mind that within the more collaborative context of supervision, we might hear concerns supervisees felt unable to discuss with their manager, that as outsiders we may be aware of issues insiders cannot see, and that we are only party to the issues supervisees choose to bring to supervision.

Challenges that are more particular to group supervision include how to:

- Ensure that the views of each person are respected.
- Create an atmosphere of collaboration and avoid escalating splits when there are grievances within the group.
- Bring the discussion back on course when disharmony erupts.
- Remain alert to the possibility of scapegoating when tensions erupt.

Supervisors carry responsibility for the structure and process of sessions; supervisees' professional development; holding group dynamics in mind as well as creating an atmosphere that is caring as well as challenging; summarizing, re-framing and challenging well-meaning but clumsy or judgemental responses; and framing concerns arising from one supervisee's experience in terms of a theme others are able to relate to. Most of us find it easier to accept feedback, even negative feedback, when the relationship is collaborative. However, even if the ethos is collaborative, because supervisors are expected to have greater expertise and experience, the relationship is inherently hierarchical.

Power and prejudice

One of the more complicated aspects of health care work relates to experiences of power and prejudice. Increased recognition of the inequities in care has led to the establishment of a wide range of initiatives aimed at promoting greater respect for religious and cultural beliefs, and fostering an environment in which diversity is seen as beneficial. However, to date, very little attention has been paid to the prejudice to which the providers of health care are exposed.

The situations might be different in other countries but in Britain the disproportionate number of people (particularly women) from ethnic minority groups working in the more vulnerable and less highly paid sectors of the National Health System (NHS) suggests that ethnic, racialized and gendered inequalities have a significant impact on the experiences of health care professionals (Gulland, 2001; Henry, 2006). In addition, although more women are entering the medical profession than before, positions of power still tend to be held by men; female doctors continue to experience prejudicial treatment and the constructs that dominate health care practice remain based on masculine models of interacting. Indeed, a recent study suggests that male and female doctors with identical experience and expertise are paid differently, that the pay gap increases the longer consultants work, and that male managers tend to take advantage of the poorer negotiating power of women with children (Connolly and Holdcroft, 2009).

Medicine is unusual as it combines power and high status with the provision of intimate care. Despite significant shifts in gendered assumptions, technical knowledge continues to be more firmly associated with men, and emotional or relational language and care giving with women. This suggests women may need to guard against assuming too much responsibility, and ensure that responding at an intimate level does not cloud objectivity and professional restraint, and men against becoming overly engaged with the technical aspects of care and providing insufficient emotional support.

It is hoped the increased numbers of women entering the medical profession will result in positions of power being less stratified according to gender, prioritizing more egalitarian relationships with patients, showing greater levels of empathy and an increased commitment to integrating work with family life. However, the answer is unlikely to lie in replacing one system of values or prejudices with another. Moreover, many assumptions of what is 'natural' to men and women are not only unfounded but reify patterns of prejudice. This is not only problematic for women: the assumption that women are more 'natural caregivers' means that men often feel their capacity to provide intimate care is undervalued and, in the case of male nurses, that their desire to work in this area is viewed with suspicion.

Supervision offers a valuable context for addressing experiences of power and prejudice. This includes voicing our commitment to anti-sexist, anti-racist and anti-homophobic practice at the outset and framing the need to remain alert to questions of diversity and power as a responsibility that is shared. Supervision also offers a context for discussing research and clinical papers that focus on the impact of sexism, racism and homophobia on experiences of health care, as well as experiential exercises aimed at increasing awareness of these issues. One such exercise involves asking people to design a 'bumper sticker' that reflects the assumptions that dominated their own family. This may require two stickers: one that reflects the dominant stories, and the other, the stories that tend to be subjugated.

It can also be helpful to treat questions of difference, power and prejudice as key themes when discussing family genograms, and ask supervisees to consider how they inform such practices as:

- The distance they put between themselves and others.
- Interactions with patients, colleagues and people in positions of authority.
- Readiness to hear, accept and engage with what is said.

However, in each case it is important to relate these experiences to the challenges supervisees face in their clinical work. For example, Megan, a hospice-based palliative care consultant, referred repeatedly to the difficulties of persuading colleagues of the importance of withstanding pressure from families to operate when a loved one is dying. In trying to help her reflect on interactions with these colleagues, the work included exploring exceptions to this 'rule', for example, whether there were any colleagues who might share or were more likely to appreciate her concerns, and what needed to happen for her voice to be heard in a different way.

Because Megan drew on gendered terms in discussing her struggle it seemed important to acknowledge gendered inequalities in the wider health care service and reflect on the impact this might have on the providers and recipients of health care. However, as comments like saying she was being treated like a 'little girl' by 'this inner sanctum of men in dark suits' suggested a more personal connection, it seemed important to ask her about gendered positions in her family. Recalling her struggles to be heard and respected by her father, and desire to adopt his more powerful role rather than replicating the position of her more subservient mother, led to the realization that feeling unheard by her colleagues tended to re-evoke her sense of being unheard by her father. Like many other palliative care consultants, Megan continues to find it extremely distressing when unnecessary intervention means that families' last days together are more difficult than need be. However, reflecting on these links seemed to free her to act differently.

Nonetheless, it is important to avoid pushing people into sharing aspects of their lives and exposing experiences they would prefer not to discuss, particularly in a group setting. With this in mind, it can be helpful to address issues of diversity at one remove. In supervising a group of colleagues, I became aware that Hitesh said far less than others and used supervision to present stories of success rather than situations he found troubling. Because he was a relatively new member of the team and the only visible member of an ethnic minority group, I was unsure of how to address this as I assumed he might feel he was at greater risk of being found wanting. In this case, a discussion about a migrant family offered a context for encouraging the group to reflect on their own experiences of 'outsiderness' and the ways in which this affects their readiness to express their views and experience of working with people who are at greater risk of prejudicial treatment. Rather than retaining an outsider position, I drew on my experience of migration and racialization. This led to a wider discussion about racialization, homophobia and other experiences of diversity, with one supervisee expressing concerns about the ways in which people with a history of alcohol abuse and mental health problems were treated within the service.

My own experience suggests that it can be more difficult to confront prejudice when this relates to one's own position. I remember, as a relatively inexperienced supervisor, being unable to say anything when a supervisee who did not know I was Jewish made an anti-Semitic comment about the people she was seeing. I suspect I remained silent because I could not trust myself to say anything without coming across as defensive or attacking. In this case, my silence meant that it was left to another supervisee to challenge what had been said. If no one had said anything, my silence would have conveyed the message that these thoughts were shared and accepted.

However, dilemmas about whether to speak out or remain silent, and how to pace what we say, are not particular to experiences of prejudice or supervision: as reflected in discussing conversations about illness, disclosure, death and blame, they are an integral aspect of health care.

Summary

- Ongoing exposure to illness, disability and death confronts health care professionals with our own mortality and limitations.

- As many of the stresses professionals face relate to external phenomena, it is important to explore ways of minimizing these stressors or responding differently.
- As some of this stress relates to our more personal experiences it is important to disentangle thoughts and feelings that relate to the professional from the more personal.
- Maintaining a greater sense of distance from the people we work with can be protective. However, this can be exhausting, is often impossible and tends to increase the sense of powerlessness being ill presents.
- Supervision has a critically important role to play in the professional development and support of health care professionals.
- Because professionals are rarely given a chance to make sense of the complex non-clinical challenges they face, although there are times when a more didactic approach is needed, and regardless of their level of experience, they are likely to benefit from reflexive forms of supervision.

APPENDIX:
SYMBOLS FOR GENOGRAMS[1]

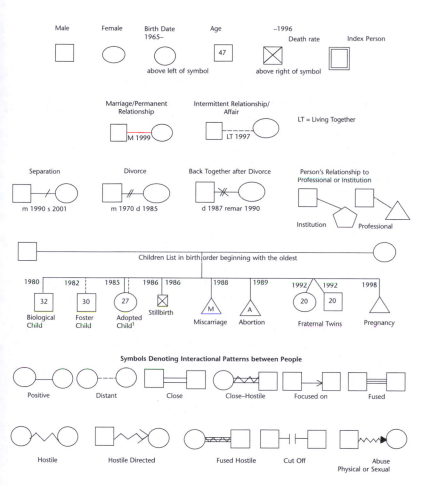

Adoption can be depicted by drawing the birth family alongside the adopted family and linking the child to both. Words, shading or symbols can also be inserted to denote other issues that seem particularly relevant, for example, illness, disability, significant mental problems, drug or alcohol abuse, cultural or ethnic identification (particularly where there are differences within the family).

1. Adapted from Power (1992).

ENDNOTES

Notes to Chapter 1

1. To avoid implying illness is the primary aspect of people's identity, unless grammatically inappropriate, instead of 'the patient', I tend to uses such terms as 'people who are ill'.
2. Although the terms 'comply' and 'adhere' tend to be used interchangeably, because 'comply' suggests obedience to authority and fails to take account of the interactional nature of experiences of health care, the term 'adhere' is used throughout this book.

Notes to Chapter 2

1. Although I have chosen to use 'parent' to refer to the child's primary care-taker, it is important to acknowledge that this does not fit for a significant proportion of children, particularly those affected by the HIV/AIDs pandemic and war.
2. Although most of the illness literature focuses on people who are married, as this does not apply to many people, the term 'partner' is used rather than 'spouse', 'husband' or 'wife'.

Note to Chapter 3

1. Adapted from Miller and Rollnick (2002, p. 79).

Note to Chapter 4

1. Although many of the challenges children and adolescents face differ, as there are considerable overlaps, the term 'children' is used to refer to both groups of people.

Notes to Chapter 10

1. Adapted from Machin (2009).
2. Adapted from Rolland (1994).
3. Adapted from Machin (2009).
4. Adapted from Gorell Barnes et al. (2000), Graff et al. (2003) and Proctor (2000).

REFERENCES

Adam, M. (2009) 'The Power of the Genogram', *Context* 109(210), 30–2.

Adams, R. G.; Blieszner, R. and de Vries, B. (2000) 'Definitions of Friendship in the Third Age: Age, Gender, and Study Location Effects', *Journal of Aging Studies* 14(1), 117–33.

Altschuler, J. (2008) 'Migration, the Family and Apartheid: Journeys that Span Geographic Space, the Life Course and Responses to Political Change', PhD Thesis, Open University, Milton Keynes.

Altschuler, J. and Dale, B. (1999) 'On Being an Ill Parent', *Journal of Clinical Child Psychology and Psychiatry* 4, 23–37.

Altschuler, J.; Dale, B. and Sass-Booth, A. (1999) 'Supporting Children when a Parent is Physically Ill: Implications for Schools', *Educational Psychology in Practice* 15(1), 25–32.

Alvarez, M. (1999) 'The Experience of Migration: A Relational Approach in Therapy', *Journal of Feminist Therapy* 11(1), 1–29.

Anderson, J. and Giest Martin, P. (2003) 'Narratives and Healing: Exploring One Family's Stories of Cancer Survivorship', *Health Communication* 15(2), 134–43.

Anderson, T. (1987) 'The Reflecting Team: Dialogue and Meta-Dialogue in Clinical Practice', *Family Process* 26, 415–28.

Anderson, W. T. (1997) 'Dying and Death in Intergenerational Families', in Hargrave, T. D. and Hanna, M. S. (eds) *The Aging Family: New Visions of Theory, Practice and Reality*. New York: Brunner/Mazel.

Anionwu, E. N. (1996) 'Ethnic Origin of Thalassaemia and Sickle Cell Counsellors', in Kelleher, D. and Hillier, S. (eds) *Researching Cultural Differences in Health*. London: Routledge.

Arad, D. (2002) 'If Your Mother Was an Animal, What Animal Would She Be? Creating Play-Stories in Family Therapy: The Animal Attribution Story-Telling Technique', *Family Process* 43(2), 249–63.

Armsden, G. C. and Lewis, F. M. (1994) 'Behavioural Adjustment and Self-esteem of School-age Children of Mothers with Breast Cancer', *Oncology Nursing Forum* 1(1), 39–45.

Asendorpf, J. P. and Wilpers, S. (2000) 'Attachment Security and Available Support: Closely Linked Relationship Qualities', *Journal of Social and Personal Relationships* 17, 115–38.

Balint, M. (1993) *The Doctor, the Patient and the Group* (2nd edition). Oxford: Churchill Livingstone.

REFERENCES

Bannon, M. J. and Ross, E. M. (1998) 'Administration of Medicines in School: Who is Responsible?' *British Medical Journal* 316, 1591–3.

Barlow, J.; Wright, C.; Sheasby, J.; Turner, A. et al. (2002) 'Self-management Approaches for People with Chronic Conditions: a Review', *Patient Education and Counseling* 48(2), 177–87.

Barnes, J.; Kroll, L.; Burke, O.; Lee, J.; Jones, A. and Stein, A. (2000) 'Qualitative Interview Study of Communication between Parents and Children about Maternal Breast Cancer', *British Medical Journal* 321(7259), 479–82.

Bateson, G. (1972) *Steps to an Ecology of Mind: Mind and Nature.* New York: Ballantine Books.

Beale, E. A.; Sivesind, E. and Bruera, D. (2004) 'Parents Dying of Cancer and their Children', *Palliative & Supportive Care* 2(4), 387–93.

Benbow, S. M. (2005) 'Gender Issues in Therapy with Later Life Families', *Context* 77, 3–6.

Benjamin, J. (1998) *Shadow of the Other: Intersubjectivity and Gender in Psychoanalysis.* London: Routledge.

Berg, C. A. and Upchurch, R. (2007) 'A Developmental-contextual Model of Couples Coping with Chronic Illness Across the Adult Life Span', *Psychological Bulletin* 133(6), 920–54.

Bloomquist, K. B.; Brown, G.; Peerson, A. and Presler, E. P. (1998) 'Transitioning to Independence: Challenges for Young People with Disabilities and their Caregivers', *Orthopaedic Nursing*, 27–35.

Bluebond-Langer, M. (1978) *The Private Worlds of Dying Children.* Princeton, NJ: Princeton University Press.

Bogo, M. and McKnight, K. (2004) 'Clinical Supervision in Social Work: a Review of the Research Literature', in Shulman, L. (ed.) *Supervision in Counselling.* New York: Haworth Press.

Boscolo, L.; Cecchin, G.; Hoffman, L. and Papp, P. (1987) *Milan Systemic Therapy: Conversations in Theory and Practice.* New York: Basic Books.

Boss, P. (2006) *Loss, Trauma and Resilience: Therapeutic Work with Ambiguous Loss.* New York: W. W. Norton.

Bowen, M. (1978) *Family Therapy in Clinical Practice.* Northvale, NJ: Jason Aronson.

Bowlby, J. (1953) *Child Care and the Growth of Love.* London: Penguin Books.

Bowlby, J. (1980) *Attachment and Loss*, vol. 3. Harmondsworth: Penguin Books.

Brennan, J. H. and Moynihan, C. (2004) *Cancer in Context.* Oxford: Oxford University Press.

Brewer, L. (2001) 'Gender Socialization and the Cultural Construction of Elder Caregivers', *Journal of Aging Studies* 15(3), 217–35.

Brom, D. and Kleber, R. (2008) 'Resilience as the Capacity for Processing Traumatic Experiences', in Brom, D.; Pat-Horenczyk, R. and Ford, J. D. *Treating Traumatized Children.* London: Routledge.

Broome, M. E. and Powell Stuart, W. (2005) 'Interventions with Families of an Acutely or Chronically Ill Child', in Crane, D. R. and Marshall, E. S. *Handbook of Families and Health.* London: Sage.

Brown, R. T. (2004) *Handbook of Pediatric Psychology in the School Setting.* Mahwah, NJ: Lawrence Erlbaum Associates.

Brown, R. T.; Wiener, L.; Kupt, M. J.; Behrman, R.; Brennen, T. et al. (2007) 'Single Parents of Children with Chronic Illness: an Understudied Phenomenon', *Journal of Pediatric Psychology* 33, 408–21.

Bruner, J. (1990) *Acts of Meaning*. Boston, MA: Harvard University Press.

Burck, C. (2005) *Multilingual Living: Explorations of Language and Subjectivity*. Basingstoke: Palgrave Macmillan.

Burnham, J. (2005) 'Relational Reflexivity: a Tool for Socially Constructing Therapeutic Relationships', in Flascos, C.; Mason, B. and Perlesz, A. (eds) *The Space Between: Experience, Context and Process in Therapeutic Relationships*. London: Karnacs.

Bury, M. (1982) 'Chronic Illness as Biographical Disruption', *Sociology of Health and Illness* 4(2), 167–82.

Butler, R. N.; Lewis, M. I. and Sunderland, T. (1991) *Aging and Mental Health: Positive Psychosocial and Biomedical Approaches*. Columbus, OH: Charles E. Merrill.

Byng-Hall, J. (1985) 'The Family Script: a Useful Bridge between Theory and Practice', *Journal of Family Therapy* 7, 301–5.

Byng-Hall, J. (1995) *Rewriting Family Scripts*. New York: Guilford Press.

Callaghan, M.; Ford, N. and Schneider, H. (2010) 'A Systematic Review of Task-shifting for HIV Treatment and Care in Africa', *Human Resources for Health* 8, 8.

Cameron, D. (2005) 'Multi-family Groups', *Context* 77, 23–6.

Campbell, D.; Draper, R. and Huffington, C. (1989) *A Systemic Approach to Consultation*. London: Karnac Books.

Campbell, T.; Griffiths, J.; Beer, H.; Tungana, J.; Bostock, V. and Parrett, N. (2011) 'A Group Approach to Facilitate Family-focused Coping with HIV+ African Parents in London', *Clinical Psychology Forum* 220, 31–6.

Campbell, T. L. (2003) 'The Effectiveness of Family Interventions for Physical Disorders', *Journal of Marital and Family Therapy* 29(2), 263–81.

Candib, L. (2002) 'Truth Telling and Advance Planning at the End of Life: Problems with Autonomy in a Multicultural World', *Families, Systems and Medicine* 20, 213–28.

Carol, J. (1995) 'Non-directive Play Therapy with Bereaved Children', in Smith, S. C. and Pennells, M. (eds) *Interventions with Bereaved Children*. London: Jessica Kingsley.

Caron, W. A. (1997) *Family Systems and Nursing Home Systems: An Ecosystemic Perspective for the Systems Practitioner*. New York: Brunner/Mazel.

Carter, B. and McGoldrick, M. (2005) *The Expanded Family Life Cycle: Individual, Family and Social Perspectives*. Boston: Allyn & Bacon.

Chamberlain, M. and Leydesdorff, S. (2004) 'Transnational Families: Memories and Narratives', *Global Networks* 4(3), 227–41.

Cheston, R. (2005) 'Shame and Avoidance: Issues of Remembering and Forgetting with People with Dementia', *Context* 77, 19–23.

Christ, G. (2000) *Healing Children's Grief: Surviving a Parent's Death from Cancer*. Oxford: Oxford University Press.

Christ, G. K.; Siegel, K. and Sperber, D. (1994) 'Impact of Parental Terminal Cancer on Adolescents', *American Journal of Orthopsychiatry* 64, 604–13.

Clay, D. L.; Cortina, S.; Harper, D. C.; Cocco, K. M. and Drotar, D. (2004) 'Schoolteachers' Experiences with Childhood Chronic Illness', *Children's Health Care* 33(3), 227–39.

Cluver, L. D.; Gardner, F. and Operario, D. (2008) 'Effects of Stigma on the Mental Health of Adolescents Orphaned by AIDS', *Journal of Adolescent Health* 42, 410–17.

Coker, N. (2001) *Racism in Medicine: Agenda for Change*. London: King's Fund.

Coles, R. L. (2001) 'Elderly Narrative Reflections on the Contradictions in Turkish Village Family Life after Migration of Adult Children', *Journal of Aging Studies* 15, 383–406.

Collins, N. L. and Feeney, B. C. (2004) 'An Attachment Theory Perspective on Closeness and Intimacy', in Mashek, D. J. and Aron, A. (eds) *Handbook of Closeness and Intimacy*. Mahwah, NJ: Lawrence Erlbaum Associates.

Combrinck-Graham, L. A. (1985) 'A Developmental Model for Family Systems', *Family Process* 24(3), 139–50.

Compass, B. E.; Worsham, N. L.; Epping-Jordan, J. E.; Grant, K. E ; Mireault, G.; Howell, D. C. and Malcarne, V. L. (1994) 'When Mom or Dad has Cancer: Markers of Psychological Distress in Cancer Patients, Spouses, and Children', *Health Psychology* 13, 507–15.

Connolly, S. and Holdcroft, A. (2009) 'The Pay Gap for Women in Medicine and Academic Medicine', *BMA Report: Women's Medical Federation*.

Cousins, R.; Davies, A. D.; Turnball, C. J. and Playfer, J. R. (2002) 'Assessing Caregiver Stress: a Conceptual Analysis and Brief Scale', *British Journal of Clinical Psychology* 41, 387–403.

Coyle J. (1999) 'Exploring the Meaning of "Dissatisfaction" with Health Care: the Importance of "Personal Identity Threat" ', *Sociology of Health and Illness* 21, 95–124.

Craig, G. M. (2007) ' "Nation", "Migration" and Tuberculosis', *Social Theory & Health* 5, 267–84.

Crombie, A. and Franklin, P. (2006) 'Family Issues in Living Donation', *Mortality* 11(2), 196–210.

Currier, J. M.; Holland, J. M. and Neimeyer, R. A. (2007) 'The Effectiveness of Bereavement Intervention with Children: a Meta-analytic Review of Controlled Outcome Research', *Journal of Clinical Child and Adolescent Psychology* 36(2), 253–9.

Curtis, E. A. and Dixon, M. S. (2005) 'Family Therapy and Systemic Practice with Older People: Where are we Now?' *Journal of Family Therapy* 27, 43–64.

Dahl, R. E. (2004) 'Adolescent Brain Development: a Period of Vulnerabilities and Opportunities', *Annals of the New York Academy of Sciences* 1021, 1–22.

Dale, B. (1997) 'Parenting and Chronic Illness', in Altschuler, J. *Working with Chronic Illness*. Basingstoke: Macmillan.

Davey, M.; Askew, J. and Godette, K. (2003) 'Parent and Adolescent Responses to Non-terminal Parental Cancer', *Families, Systems and Health* 21(3), 245–58.

Davies, B. and Harre, R. (1999) 'Positioning and Personhood', in van Langenhove, L. and Harre, R. (eds) *Positioning Theory*. Oxford: Blackwell.

Davies, S. and Nolan, M. (2003) ' "Making the Best of Things": Relatives' Experience of Decisions about Care-home Entry', *Aging and Society* 23(4), 429–50.

de Graaff, F. M. and Francke, A. L. (2009) 'Barriers to Home Care for Terminally Ill Turkish and Moroccan Migrants, Perceived by GPs and Nurses: a Survey', *BioMed Central Palliative Care* 8(3).

de Mol, J. and Buysse, A. (2008) 'The Phenomenology of Children's Influence on Parents', *Journal of Family Therapy* 30(2), 163–93.

Department of Health (2001) 'National Service Framework for Older People', www.dh.gov.uk/en/Publicationsandstatistics/Publications/PublicationsPolicy AndGuidance/DH_4003066

Specification for the Commissioner-led Pathfinder Programme, London.

Department of Health (2010) *Understanding the Health Needs of Migrants in the South East Region*, A Report by the South East Migrant Health Study Group on behalf of the Department of Health.

DFES-1448 (2005) *Managing Medicines in Schools and Early Years Settings*.Online publications for schools.

Doka, K. J. (1999) 'Disenfranchised Grief', *Bereavement Care* 18(3), 37–9.

Down, G. (2010) 'Relationships between Healthcare Staff and Families in a Paediatric Hospital: a Grounded Theory Study', *Human Systems* 21(2), 237–69.

Dyson, S. M.; Culley, L. A.; Gill, C.; Hubbard, S.; Kennefick, A.; Morris, P.; Rees, D.; Sutton, F. and Squire, P. (2006) 'Ethnicity Questions and Antenatal Screening for Sickle Cell/Thalassaemia [EQUANS] in England: a Randomized Controlled Trial of Two Questionnaires', *Ethnicity and Health* 11(2), 169–89.

Edwards, B. and Clarke, V. (2004) 'The Psychological Impact of a Cancer Diagnosis on Families: the Influence of Family Functioning and Patients' Illness Characteristics on Depression and Anxiety', *Psycho-Oncology* 13(8), 562–76.

Edwards, R.; Hadfield, J.; Lucey, H. and Mauthner, M. (2006) *Sibling Identity and Relationships: Sisters and Brothers*. London: Routledge.

Eiser, C. (1997) 'Effects of Chronic Illness on Children and their Families', *Advances in Psychiatric Treatment* 3, 204–10.

Ell, R. K. O.; Nishimoto, H.; Mantell, J. E. and Homovitz, M. B. (1998) 'Psychological Adaptation to Cancer: a Comparison among Patients, Spouses and Nonspouses', *Family Systems Medicine* 6(3), 335–48.

Escot, C.; Artero, S.; Boulanger, J. P. and Ritchie, K. (2001) 'Stress Levels in Nursery Staff Working in Oncology', *Stress and Health* 17, 273–9.

Falicov, C. (1998) *Latino Families in Therapy*. New York: Guilford Press.

Famuyiwa, O. O. and Akinyanju, O. O. (1998) 'Burden of Sickle Cell Anaemia on Families of Patients', *International Journal of Social Psychiatry* 44(3), 170–80.

Field, M. J. and Behrman, R. E. (2003) *When Children Die: Improving Palliative and End-of-life Care for Children and their Families*. Washington, DC: National Academies Press.

Firth, P. (2003) 'Multi-professional Team Work', in Monroe, B. and Olivier, D. (eds) *Patient Participation in Palliative Care: A Voice for the Voiceless*. Oxford: Oxford University Press.

Firth-Cozens, J. (2003) 'Doctors, their Wellbeing, and their Stress', *British Medical Journal* 326, 670–1.

Flascos, C. and Pocock, D. (2009) *Systems and Psychoanalysis: Contemporary Integrations in Family Therapy*. London: Karnac Books.

Flores, G. (2000) 'Culture and the Patient–Physician Relationship: Achieving Cultural Competency in Health Care', *Journal of Pediatrics* 136(1), 4–23.

Fobair, P.; O'Hanlon, K.; Koopman, C.; Classen, C.; Dimiceli, S.; Drooker, N. et al. (2001) 'Comparison of Lesbian and Heterosexual Women's Response to Newly Diagnosed Breast Cancer', *Psycho-Oncology* 10, 40–51.

Folkman, S. (1997) 'Positive Psychological States and Coping with Severe Stress', *Social Science Medicine* 45, 1207–21.

Frankl, V. (1984) *Man's Search for Meaning: An Introduction to Logotherapy*. New York: Touchstone.

Fredman, G. (1997) *Death Talk: Conversations with Children and Families*. London: Karnac Books.

Fredman, G.; Christie, D. and Bear, N. (2007) 'Reflecting Teams with Children: the Bear Necessities', *Clinical Child Psychology and Psychiatry* 12(2), 211–22.

Freud, S. (1917) *Mourning and Melancholia*, XVII (2nd edition, 1955). London: Hogarth Press.

Frosh, S.; Phoenix, A. and Pattman, R. (2002) *Young Masculinities: Understanding Boys in Contemporary Society*. London: Palgrave Macmillan.

Gabriel, S. E. (1999) 'The Epidemiology of Gender-discrepant Illness', *Lupus* 8, 339–45.

Gabriels, R. L.; Wamboldt, D. R.; McCormick, D. R.; Adams, T. L. and McTaggart, S. R. (2000) 'Children's Illness Drawings and Asthma Symptom Awareness', *Journal of Asthma* 37(7), 565–74.

Gandhi, I. G.; Parle, J. V.; Greenfield, S. M. and Gould, S. (1997) 'A Qualitative Investigation into Why Patients Change their GPs', *Family Practice* 14, 49–57.

Gerhardt, C.; Vannatta, K.; McKellop, M.; Zeller, M.; Taylor, J.; Passo, M. et al. (2003) 'Comparing Family Functioning, Parental Distress and the Role of Social Support of Care Givers With and Without a Child with Juvenile Rheumatoid Arthritis', *Journal of Pediatric Psychology* 28, 5–15.

Gericke, A. (2002) 'Mental Health Prevention in a Target Group at Risk: Children of Somatically Ill Parents', http://cordis.europa.eu/data/PROJ_FP5/ACTIO NeqDndSESSIONeq112482005919ndDOCeq1731ndTBLeqEN_PROJ.htm

Giles, J. and Mu, R. (2005) 'Elder Parent Health and the Migration Decision of Adult Children: Evidence from Rural China', *IZA DP* 2333, 1–56.

Gilligan, C. (1982) *In a Different Voice: Psychological Theory and Women's Development*. Cambridge: Harvard University Press.

Given, C. W.; Given, B. A.; Azzouz, F.; Kozachik, S.; and Stommel, M. (2001) 'Predictors of Pain and Fatigue in the Year Following Diagnosis among Elderly Cancer Patients', *Journal of Pain and Symptom Management* 21(6), 456–66.

Goldstein, P. and Friend, S. (2009) 'Groups within Groups: a Programme for Bereaved Children', *Context* 101, 9–10.

Gorell Barnes, G.; Down, G. and McCann, D. (2000) *Systemic Supervision*. London: Jessica Kingsley.

Graff, J.; Lund-Jacobsen, D. and Wermer, A. (2003) 'X-files: The Power of Personal Stories in Private–Professional Consultation', *Human Systems* 14(1), 17–32.

Granger, E. and Baker, M. (2002) in Tribe, R. and Raval, H. (eds) *Working with Interpreters in Mental Health*. London: Bruner-Routledge.

Greeff, A. P. and Joubert, A. M. (2007) 'Spirituality and Resilience in Families in which a Parent has Died', *Psychological Reports* 100, 897–900.

Green, R. J. and Mitchell, V. (2002) 'Gay and Lesbian Couples in Therapy: Homophobia, Relational Ambiguity and Social Support', in Gurman, A. S. and Jacobson, A. S. (eds) *Clinical Handbook of Couple Therapy*. New York: Guilford Press.

Greer, S. (2000) 'Fighting Spirit in Patients with Cancer', *The Lancet* 335(9206), 847–8.

Gross, V.; McNab, S.; Altschuler, J. and Ganda, M. (2003) 'Agency Supervision – a New Module for Systemic Therapy Training', *Human Systems* 14(1), 55–66.

Gulland, A. (2001) 'Ethnic Minority Doctors Hit Glass Ceiling in NHS', *British Medical Journal* 23, 322(7301), 1505.

Harjai, K. J.; Nunez, E.; Humphrey, J. S.; Turgot, T.; Shah, M. and Newman, J. (2000) 'Does Gender Bias Exist in the Medical Management of Heart Failure?' *Cardiology* 75(1), 65–9.

Haub, C. (2007) *World Population Data Sheet*. Washington DC: Population Reference Bureau.

Helgeson, V. K. and Novak, S. A. (2006) 'Illness Centrality and Well-Being among Male and Female Early Adolescents with Diabetes', *Journal of Pediatric Psychology* 32, 3–13.

Henry, L. (2006) 'Institutional Disadvantage: Old Ghanaian Nurses' and Midwives' Reflections on Career Progression and Stagnation in the NHS', *Journal of Clinical Nursing* Special Issue.

Herbert, E. and Carpenter, B. (2007) 'Fathers – the Secondary Partners: Professional Perceptions and a Father's Recollections', *Children and Society* 8(1), 31–41.

Herman, J. (1997) *Trauma and Recovery*. New York: Basic Books.

Hill, S. and Zimmerman, M. (1995) 'Valiant Girls and Vulnerable Boys: the Impact of Gender and Race on Mothers' Caregiving for Chronically-Ill Children', *Journal of Marriage and the Family* 57, 43–53.

Hillier, S. and Kelleher, D. (1996) 'Considering Culture, Ethnicity and the Politics of Health', in Kelleher, D. and Hillier, S. (eds) *Researching Cultural Differences in Health*. London: Routledge.

Hirschman, O. (1970) *Exit, Voice and Loyalty: Responses to Decline in Firms, Organizations and States*. Cambridge, MA: Harvard University Press.

Hodern, D. J. and Currow, D. C. (2003) 'A Patient-centred Approach to Sexuality in the Face of Life-limiting Illness', *Palliative Care* 179, 8–11.

Hoffman, L. (1993) *Exchanging Voices: A Collaborative Approach to Therapy*. London: Karnac Books.

Hoke, L. A. (2001) 'Psychosocial Adjustment in Children of Mothers with Breast Cancer', *Psycho-Oncology* 10, 361–9.

Hollway, W. (1984) 'Gender Difference and the Production of Subjectivity', in Henriques, W.; Hollway, W.; Urwin, C.; Venn, C. and Walkerdine, V. (eds) *Changing the Subject*. London: Methuen.

REFERENCES

Hopkins, R. (2002) 'Narrative, Culture and Power: a Systemic Perspective on Cross-Cultural Communication in General Practice', Master's Thesis, Tavistock Clinic.

Hughes, N.; Closs, S. J. and Clark, D. (2009) 'Experiencing Cancer in Old Age: a Qualitative Systematic Review', *Qualitative Health Research* 19(8), 1139–53.

Imber-Black, E. (2004) 'Rituals and the Healing Process', in Walsh, F. and McGoldrick, M. (eds) *Living Beyond Loss: Death in the Family*. London: W. W. Norton.

Iveson, C. (2001) *Whose Life? Working with Older People*. London: BT Press.

Jenkins, R. A. and Pargamet, K. I. (1995) 'Religion and Spirituality as Resources for Coping with Cancer', *Journal of Psychosocial Oncology* 13(1), 51–74.

Joffe, H. (2007) 'Anxiety, Mass Crisis and "the Other" ', in Perri 6; Radstone, S.; Squire, C. and Treacher, A. (eds) *Public Emotions*. London: Palgrave Macmillan.

Jones, D. and Paramjit, S. G. (1998) 'Refugees and Primary Care: Tackling the Inequalities', *British Medical Journal* 317, 1444–6.

Judd, D. (1989) *Give Sorry Words: Working with a Dying Child*. London: Free Association Books.

Karim, K.; Bailey, M. J. and Tunna, K. (2000) 'Non-white Ethnicity and the Provision of Palliative Care Services: Factors Affecting Doctors' Referral Patterns', *Palliative Medicine* 14, 471–8.

Kayser, K.; Watson, L. E. and Anrade, J. L. (2007) 'Cancer as a "We-Disease": Examining the Process of Coping from a Relational Perspective', *Family Systems and Health* 25(4), 404–18.

Kazak, A. (2006) 'Pediatric Psychosocial Preventative Health Model (PPPHM): Research, Practice and Collaboration in Pediatric Family Systems Medicine', *Family Systems and Health* 24(4), 381–95.

Kazak, A.; Simons, S.; Alderfer, M. A.; Rourke, M. T.; Crump, T.; McClure, K.; Jones, P.; Rodriguez, A.; Boeving, A.; Whang, W.-T. and Reilly, A. (2005) 'Feasibility and Preliminary Outcomes from a Pilot Study of a Brief Psychological Intervention for Families of Children Newly Diagnosed with Cancer', *Journal of Pediatric Psychology* 30(8), 644–55.

Keicolt-Glaser, J. K. and Newton, T. L. (2001) 'Marriage and Health: His and Hers', *Psychological Bulletin* 127, 472–503.

Kilminster, S. M. and Jolly, B. C. (2000) 'Effective Supervision in Clinical Practice Settings: a Literature Review', *Medical Education* 34, 827–40.

Klein, M. (1975) *Envy and Gratitude and Other Works*. New York: Delta.

Kleinman, A. (1998) *The Illness Narratives: Suffering, Healing and the Human Condition*. London: Basic Books.

Kleinman, A.; Eisenberg, L. and Good, B. (2006) 'Culture, Illness, and Care: Clinical Lessons from Anthropologic and Cross-Cultural Research', *Focus* 4, 140–9.

Knafil, K. A. and Gillis, C. L. (2002) 'Families and Chronic Illness: a Synthesis of Current Research', *Journal of Family Nursing* 8(3), 178–98.

Koenig, H. K.; Larson, D. B. and Larson, S. S. (2001) 'Religion and Coping with Serious Medical Illness', *The Annals of Pharmacotherapy* 35(3), 352–9.

Koopmans, G. T. and Lamers, L. M. (2007) 'Gender and Health Care Utilization: the Role of Mental Distress and Help-seeking Propensity', *Social Science and Medicine* 64(6), 1216–30.

Koplow, L. and Messenger, E. (1990) 'Developmental Dilemmas of Young Children of Immigrant Parents', *Child and Adolescent Social Work Journal* 7(2), 121–34.

Krause, I. B. (1998) *Therapy Across Culture*. London: Sage.

Kriseman, N. L. and Claes, J. A. (1997) 'Gender Issues and Elder Care', in Hargrave, T. D. and Hanna, M. S. (eds) *The Aging Family: New Visions of Theory, Practice and Reality*. New York: Brunner/Mazel.

Kristofferzon, M.; Lofmark, R. and Carlsson, M. (2003) 'Myocardial Infarction: Gender Differences in Coping and Social Support', *Journal of Advanced Nursing* 44(4), 360–74.

Kubler-Ross, E. (1970) *On Death and Dying*. London: Tavistock.

Lansdown, R. and Benjamin, G. (1985) 'The Development of the Concept of Death in Children aged 5–9 Years', *Child: Care Health Development* 11, 13–20.

Last, B. F.; Groontehuis, M. A.; and Eiser, C. (2005) 'International Comparison of Contributions to Psychosocial Research on Survivors of Childhood Cancer: Past and Future Considerations', *Journal of Pediatric Psychology* 30(1), 99–113.

Launer, J. and Halpern, H. (2006) 'Reflective Practice and Clinical Supervision: an Approach to Promoting Clinical Supervision among General Practitioners', *Workbased Learning in Primary Care* 4, 69–72.

Lavee, Y. and May-Dan, M. (2003) 'Patterns of Change of Marital Relationships among Parents of Children with Cancer', *Health Social Work* 28, 255–63.

Lavelle, K.; Todd, C.; Moran, A.; Howell, A.; Bundred, A. and Campbell, M. (2007) 'Non-standard Management of Breast Cancer Increases with Age in the UK: a Population Based Cohort of Women ≥ 65 Years', *British Journal of Cancer* 96(8), 1197–203.

Lee, R. E. and Dwyer, T. (1995) 'Co-constructed Narratives around Being "Sick": a Minimalist Model', *Contemporary Family Therapy* 17(1), 65–82.

Leichtentritt, R. D. and Rettig, K. D. (2000) 'Elderly Israelis and their Family Members' Meaning towards Euthanasia', *Families, Systems and Health* 18(1), 61–79.

Le Shan, L. (1989) *Cancer as a Turning Point: A Handbook for People with Cancer, Their Families, and Health Professionals*. New York: Penguin.

Lester, R. T.; Ritvo, P.; Mills, E. J.; Kariri, A.; Karanja, S.; Chung, M. H. et al. (2010) 'Effects of a Mobile Phone Short Messaging Service on Antiretroviral Treatment Adherence in Kenya: a Randomized Trial', *Lancet* 376(9755), 1838–45.

Lévi-Strauss, C. (1987) *Introduction to Marcel Mauss*. London: Routledge.

Lintz, K. C.; Penson, R. T.; Chabner, B. A. and Lynch, T. J. (1998) 'A Staff Dialogue on Caring for an Intensely Spiritual Patient: Psychosocial Issues Faced by Patients, Their Families, and Caregivers', *The Oncologist* 3(6), 439–45.

Little, M.; Paul, K.; Jordens, C. F. C. and Sayers, E. J. (2002) 'Survivorship and Discourses of Identity', *Psycho-Oncology* 11, 170–8.

Lobato, D. and Kao, B. T. (2002) 'Integrated Sibling–Parent Group Intervention to Improve Sibling Knowledge and Adjustment to Chronic Illness and Disability', *Society of Pediatric Psychology* 27(8), 711–16.

Long, J. (1997) 'Alzheimer's Disease and the Family: Working with New Realities', in Hargrave, T. D. and Hanna, S. (eds) *The Aging Family: New Visions of Theory, Practice and Reality*. New York: Brunner/Mazel.

Long, T.; Sque, M. and Addington-Hall, J. (2008) 'Conflict Rationalization: How Family Members Cope with a Diagnosis of Brain Stem Cell Death', *Social Science and Medicine* 67(2), 253–61.

Lorber, J. and Moore, L. J. (2002) *Gender and the Social Construction of Illness*. New York: Alta Mira Press.

Machin, L. (2009) *Working with Loss and Grief*. London: Sage.

Manne, S. L. (1998) 'Cancer in the Marital Context: a Review of the Literature', *Cancer Investigation* 16, 188–202.

Manning, C. (2010) 'The Schwartz Center Rounds: Evaluation of an Interdisciplinary Approach to Enhancing Patient-Centered Communication, Teamwork, and Provider Support', *Academic Medicine* 85(8), 1073–81.

Marshall, P. A. and O'Keefe, J. P. (1995) 'Medical Students' First Person Narratives of a Patient's Story of AIDs', *Social Science and Medicine* 40(1), 67–76.

Mason, B. (2004) 'A Relational Approach to the Management of Chronic Pain', *Clinical Psychology* 35, 17–20.

Matalon, A. and Mazor, A. (1999) 'The Meaning of Balint's "Mutual Investment Company": a Family Physician's Analysis of Ten Years of Caring for a Family', *Family Systems and Health* 17, 365–72.

Mathers, N. J. and Gask, L. (1995) 'Surviving the "Heartsink" Experience', *Family Practice* 12(2), 176–83.

Mattingley, C. (1998) *Healing Dramas and Clinical Plots: The Narrative Structure of Experience*. Cambridge: Cambridge University Press.

McCann, D.; Gorrell-Barnes, G. and Down, G. (2000) 'Sex and Sexuality: the Supervisory Challenge', in Gorrell-Barnes, G.; Down, G. and McCann, D. (eds) *Systemic Supervision*. London: Jessica Kingsley.

McConkey, R. (1994) 'Early Intervention: Planning Futures, Shaping Years', *Mental Handicap Research* 7(1), 4–15.

McGoldrick, M.; Gerson, R. and Shellenberger, S. (1999) *Genograms in Family Assessment*. London: W. W. Norton.

McGrath, P.; Vun, M. and McLeod, L. (2001) 'Needs and Experiences of Non-English-speaking Hospice Patients and Families in an English-speaking Country', *American Journal of Hospital and Palliative Care* 18(5), 305–12.

McInnes, R. A. (2003) 'Chronic Illness and Sexuality', *Medical Journal Australia* 179, 263–6.

Menzies-Lyth, I. E. P. (1960) 'Social Systems as a Defence against Anxiety: an Empirical Study of the Nursing Service of a General Hospital', cited in Trist, E. and Meyerstein, I. (1994) 'Reflections on "Being there" and "Doing" in Family Therapy', *Family Systems Medicine* 12(1), 21–9.

Meyerstein, I. (1994) 'Reflections on "Being There" and "Doing" in Family Therapy', *Family Systems Medicine* 12(1), 21–9.

Militiades, H. B. (2002) 'The Social and Psychological Effect of an Adult Child's Emigration on Non-immigrant Asian Indian Elderly Parents', *Journal of Cross-Cultural Gerontology* 17, 33–55.

Miller, J. B. and Stiver, I. P. (1997) *A Relational Reframing of Therapy: Work in Progress*, Stone Paper Working Paper Series 52. Wellesley, MA.

Miller, R. B.; Hemesath, K. and Nelson, B. (1997) 'Marriage in Middle and Later Life', in Hargrave, T. D. and Hanna, S. M. (eds) *The Aging Family: New Visions of Theory, Practice and Reality*. New York: Brunner/Mazel.

Miller, S. M. (1995) 'Monitoring versus Blunting Styles of Coping with Cancer Influences the Information Patients Want and Need about their Illness', *Cancer* 76, 167–77.

Miller, W. R. and Rollnick, S. (2002) *Motivational Interviewing: Preparing People for Change*. New York: Guilford Press.

Mitchell, J. (2003) *Siblings, Sex and Violence*. Cambridge: Polity Press.

Montalvo, B.; Harmon, D. and Elliott, M. (1998) 'Family Mobilization: Work with Angry Elderly Couples in Declining Health', *Contemporary Family Therapy* 20(2), 163–73.

Morgan, J. (2001) 'Boxes and Remembering in the Time of AIDS', *AIDS Bulletin* 10, 2.

Moss, A. H.; Holley, J. L.; Davison, S. N.; Richard, A. D.; Germain, M. J.; Cohen, L. and Schwarz, R. D. (2004) 'Core Curriculum in Nephrology', *American Journal of Kidney Disease* 43(1), 172–85.

Mouratoglou, V. (2005) 'Family Therapy with Elderly People in a Hospital', *Context* 77, 9–11.

Newman, S.; Steed, L. and Mulligan, K. (2009) *Chronic Physical Illness: Self-Management and Behavioural Interventions*. Maidenhead: Open University Press.

Noll, R. B. and Kupt, M. J. (2007) 'Commentary: The Psychological Impact of Pediatric Cancer: Hardiness, the Exception of the Rule?' *Journal of Pediatric Psychology* 32(9), 1089–98.

O'Brien, I.; Dufy, H. and Nicoll, H. (2009) 'Impact of Childhood Chronic Illness on Children: a Literature Review', *British Journal of medicine* 18(32), 1358–65.

Office for National Statistics (2007) 'Social Trends', www.statistics.gov.uk/social-trends 38.

Ohman, M.; Soderberg, S. and Lundman, B. (2003) 'Hovering between Suffering and Enduring: the Meaning of Living with Serious Chronic Illness' *Qualitative Health Research* 13(4), 528–42.

Olsson, C. A.; Boyce, M. F.; Toumbourou, J. W. and Sawyer, S. M. (2005) 'The Role of Peer Support in Facilitating Psychosocial Adjustment to Chronic Illness in Adolescence', *Clinical Child Psychology and Psychiatry* 10(1), 78–87.

Pai, A.; Patino-Fernandez, A. M.; McSherry, M.; Beeld, D.; Alderfer, M.; Teilly, A. et al. (2008) 'The Psychosocial Assessment Tool (PAT2.0): Psychometric Properties of a Screener for Psychosocial Distress in Families of Children Newly Diagnosed with Cancer', *Journal of Pediatric Psychology* 33, 50–62.

Parkes, C. M. (1971) 'Psycho-social Transitions: a Field for Study', *Social Sciences and Medicine* 5, 101–15.

Parkes, C. M. (2002) 'Grief: Lessons from the Past, Visions for the Future', *Bereavement Care* 21, 19–23.

PATA (2010) 'Plenary Discussion: Working with Adolescents Affected and Infected by HIV/AIDs', *Pediatric Treatment for HIV/AIDs Conference*, Uganda.

Peres, J. P.; Moreira-Almeida, A.; Nosella, A. G. and Koenig, H. G. (2007) 'Spirituality and Resilience in Trauma Victims', *Journal of Religious Health* 46, 343–50.

Phoenix, A. and Pattyama, P. (2006) 'Intersectionality', *European Journal of Women's Studies* 13, 187–98.

Pipher, M. (1999) *Another Country*. New York: Riverhead Books.

Pitceathly, C. and Maguire, P. (2003) 'The Psychological Impact of Cancer on Patients' Partners and Other Key Relatives: a Review', *European Journal of Cancer* 39(11), 1517–24.

Power, T. A. (1992) *Family Matters: A Layperson's Guide to Family Functioning*. New Hampshire: Hathaway Press.

Proctor, B. (2000) *Group Supervision*. London: Sage.

Rathbone, J. (2009) 'Living with Terminal Illness', *Context* 101, 18–19.

Reiss, D.; Gonzalez, S. and Kramer, M. (1986) 'On the Weakness of Strong Bonds', *Archives of General Psychiatry* 43, 795–804.

Richards, H.; Reid, M. and Watt, G. (2003) 'Victim Blaming Revisited: a Qualitative Study of Beliefs about Illness Causation, and Responses to Chest Pain', *Family Practice* 20, 711–16.

Rivas, L. M. (2003) 'Invisible Labours: Caring for the Independent Person', in Ehrenreich, B. and Hochschild, A. R. (eds) *Global Woman: Nannies, Maids, and Sex Workers in the New Economy*. New York: Metropolitan Books.

Roehlkepartian, E. G.; King, E. G.; Wagener, L. and Benson, P. L. (2006) *Handbook of Spiritual Development in Childhood and Adolescence*. London: Sage.

Rolland, J. S. (1994) *Families, Illness and Disability: An Integrative Treatment Model*. New York: Basic Books.

Rolland, J. S. (2006) 'Genetics, Family Systems, and Multicultural Influences', *Families, Systems, & Health* 24(4), 425–41.

Romer, G.; Barkmann, C.; Thomalla, G. and Riedesser, P. (2002) 'Children of Somatically Ill Parents: a Methodological Review', *Clinical Child Psychology and Psychiatry* 7(1), 17–38.

Rossi, A. S. and Rossi, P. H. (1990) *Of Human Bonding: Parent–Child Relations Across the Life Course*. New York: Aldine de Gruyter.

Rowling, L. (2010) 'Schools and Grief: Attending to People and Places', in Monroe, B. and Kraus, F. (eds) *Brief Interventions with Children* (2nd edition). Oxford: Oxford University Press.

Rutter, M. (2006) 'Implications of Resilience Concepts for Scientific Understanding', *Annals of the New York Academy of Science* 1094, 1–12.

Sallfors, C. and Hallberg, L. R. R. (2003) 'A Personal Perspective on Living with a Chronically Ill Child: a Qualitative Study', *Families Systems and Health* 21(2), 193–204.

Scheppers, E.; van Dongen, E.; Dekker, J.; Geertzen, J. and Dekker, J. (2006) 'Potential Barriers to the Use of Health Services among Ethnic Minorities: a Review', *Family Practice* 23(3), 325–48.

Schmitt, F.; Manninen, H.; Santahlati, P.; Savonlahti, E.; Pyrhonen, S.; Romer, G. and Piha, J. (2007) 'Children of Parents with Cancer: a Collaborative Project between a Child Psychiatry Clinic and an Adult Oncology Clinic', *Clinical Child Psychology and Psychiatry* 12(2), 421–36.

Schofield, T.; Connell, R. W.; Walker, J.; Wood, F. and Butland, T. (2000) 'Understanding Men's Health and Illness: a Gender-relations Approach to Policy, Research, and Practice', *Journal of American College Health* 48(6), 247–56.

Seale, C. (1998) 'Demographic Change and Care of the Dying, 1969–1987', in Dickenson, D. and Johnson, M. (eds) *Death, Dying and Bereavement.* London: Sage Publications.

Seligman, L. (1996) *Promoting a Fighting Spirit: Psychotherapy for Cancer Patients, Survivors, and Their Families.* San Francisco: Jossey Bass.

Sharpe, D. and Rossiter, L. (2002) 'Siblings of Children with a Chronic Illness: a Meta-analysis', *Journal of Pediatric Psychology* 27(8), 699–710.

Shields, C. G. and Rousseau, S. L. (2004) 'A Pilot Study of an Intervention for Breast Cancer Survivors and Their Spouses', *Family Process* 43, 95–107.

Shore, A. N. (2001) 'Effects of a Secure Attachment Relationship on Right Brain Development, Affect Regulation and Infant Mental Health', *Infant Mental Health Journal* 22(1–2), 7–66.

Shotter, J. (1994) *Conversational Realities: Constructing Life through Language.* London: Sage.

Slaughter, V. and Griffiths, M. (2007) 'Death Understanding and Fear of Death in Young Children', *Clinical Child Psychology and Psychiatry* 12(4), 525–35.

Smith, T. W. and Glazer, K. M. (2006) 'Hostility, Marriage and the Heart: the Social Psychophysiology of Cardiovascular Risk in Close Relationships', in Crane, D. R. and Marshall, E. S. (eds) *Handbook of Families and Health.* London: Sage.

Sontag, S. (1991) *Illness as Metaphor and AIDS and its Metaphors.* London: Penguin Books.

Sox, C. M.; Burstin, H. R.; Orav, E. J.; Conn, A.; Setnik, G.; Rucker, D. W.; Dasse, P. and Brennan, T. A. (1998) 'The Effect of Supervision of Residents on Quality of Care in Five University-affiliated Emergency Departments', *Academy of Medicine* 73(7), 776–82.

Steinglass, P. (1998) 'Multiple Family Discussion Groups for Patients with Chronic Medical Illness', *Families, Systems and Health* 16, 55–70.

Stern, D. (1985) *The Interpersonal World of the Infant: A View from Psychoanalysis and Developmental Psychology.* New York: Basic Books.

Stockwell, P. (2005) 'Systemic Ideas and Life Story Work with Older Adults', *Context* 77, 16–18.

Stoppelbein, L. and Greening, L. (2007) 'Brief Report: The Risk of Posttraumatic Stress Disorder in Mothers of Children with Pediatric Cancer and Type I Diabetes', *Journal of Pediatric Psychology* 32(2), 223–9.

Surbone, A.; Kagawa-Singer, M.; Terret, C. and Baider, L. (2006) 'The Illness Trajectory of Elderly Cancer Patients Across Cultures: SIOG Position Paper', *Annals of Oncology* 18(4), 633–8.

Thastum, M.; Johansen, M. B.; Gubba, L.; Olesen, L. B. and Romer, G. (2008) 'Coping, Social Relations, and Communication: a Qualitative Exploratory Study of Children with Cancer', *Clinical Child Psychology and Psychiatry* 13(1), 123–38.

Thorne, T. (2005) 'The Write Stuff: Using Therapeutic Letters with Older Adults', *Context* 77, 12–15.

Tomm, K. (1988) 'Interventive Interviewing, Part III: Intending to Ask Lineal, Circular, Strategic and Reflexive Questions?' *Family Process* 27, 1–15.

Tse, C. Y.; Chong, A. and Fok, S. Y. (2003) 'Breaking Bad News: a Chinese Perspective', *Palliative Medicine* 17(4), 339–43.

Turner, J. D. (2005) 'Intimacy in Later Life', *Context* 77, 7–8.

Umberson, D. (2003) *Death of a Parent.* Cambridge: Cambridge University Press.

van der Geest, A. M.; Mul, A. and Vermeulen, H. (2004) 'Linkages between Migration and the Care of Frail Older People: Observations from Greece, Ghana and the Netherlands', *Ageing and Society* 24(3), 431–50.

van Riper, M. and Gallo, A. M. (2006) 'Families Health and Genomics', in Crane, D. R. and Marshall, E. S. (eds) *Handbook of Families and Health.* London: Sage.

Vaughan-Cole, B. (2006) 'Death, Grief and Bereavement in Families', in Crane, D. R. and Marshall, E. S. (eds) *Handbook of Families and Health.* London: Sage.

Visser, A.; Huizinga, G. A.; Hoekstra, H. J.; van der Graaf, W. T.; Klip, E. C.; Pras, E.; Hoekstra-Weebers, J. E. (2005) 'Emotional and Behavioural Functioning of Children of a Parent Diagnosed with Cancer: a Cross-informant Perspective', *Psycho-Oncology* 14, 746–58.

von Bertalanffy, L. (1968) *General Systems Theory: Foundation, Development, Application.* New York: Brazillier.

Waldron, I. (2005) 'Gender Differences in Mortality – Causes and Variation in Different Societies', in Conrad, P. (ed.) *The Sociology of Health and Illness: Critical Perspectives.* New York: St Martin's Press.

Walker, G. (1983) 'The Pact: the Caretaker-parent/Ill-child Coalition in Families with Chronic Illness', *Family Systems Medicine* 1(4), 6–29.

Walker, G. (1991) *In the Midst of Winter: Systemic Therapy with Families, Couples and Individuals with AIDS Infection.* London: W. W. Norton.

Walker, L. S. and Zeman, J. L. (1992) 'Parental Response to Child Illness Behavior', *Journal of Pediatric Psychology* 17(1), 49–71.

Walsh, F. (2004) 'Personal Reflections on Loss', in Walsh, F. and McGoldrick, M. (eds) *Living Beyond Loss: Death in the Family.* London: W. W. Norton.

Walsh, F. and McGoldrick, M. (2004) 'Loss and the Family: a Systemic Approach', in Walsh, F. and McGoldrick, M. (eds) *Living Beyond Loss: Death in the Family.* London: W. W. Norton.

Wass, H. and Myers, J. E. (1982) 'Psychosocial Aspects of Death among the Elderly: a Review of the Literature', *Personnel and Guidance* 61, 131–3.

Way, P. and Bremner, I. (2010) 'Therapeutic Interventions', in Monroe, B. and Kraus, F. (eds) *Brief Interventions with Children* (2nd edition). Oxford: Oxford University Press.

Way, P.; Kraus, F. and the Candle team (2010) 'Groupwork', in Monroe, B. and Kraus, F. (eds) *Brief Interventions with Children* (2nd edition). Oxford: Oxford University Press.

Weingarten, K. (1994) *The Mother's Voice: Strengthening Intimacy in Families.* London: Harcourt Brace.

Weingarten, K. and Worthen, M. E. (1997) 'A Narrative Approach to Understanding the Illness Experience of a Mother and Daughter', *Family Systems and Health* 15(1), 41–54.

Weingarten, K. and Worthen, M. E. (2009) 'Narrative in Action: the Daily Practice of Acknowledgement', *Context* 105, 29–32.

Weiss, R. S. (1993) 'Loss and Recovery', in Stroebe, M. S.; Stroebe, W. and Hansson, R. O. (eds) *Handbook of Bereavement: Theory, Research and Intervention*. New York: Cambridge University Press.

Welch, A. S.; Wadsworth, M. E. and Compas, B. E. (1996) 'Adjustment of Children and Adolescents to Parental Cancer', *Cancer* 77(7), 1409–18.

Wenger, G. C.; Davies, R.; Shahatahmasebi, S. and Scott, A. (1996) 'Social Isolation and Loneliness in Old Age: Review and Model Refinement', *Ageing and Society* 6, 333–58.

White, C. A. (2000) 'Body Image Dimensions and Cancer: a Heuristic Cognitive Behavioural Model', *Psycho-Oncology* 9, 183–93.

White, M. and Epston, D. (1990) *Narrative Means to Therapeutic Ends*. New York: W. W. Norton.

Wilkinson, S. M. (1995) 'The Changing Pressure for Cancer Nurses 1986–1993', *European Journal of Cancer Care* 4, 69–74.

Williams, P. D.; Williams, A. R.; Graff, J. C.; Hanson, S., et al. (2003) 'A Community-based Intervention for Siblings and Parents of Children with Chronic Illness or Disability: the ISEE Study', *Journal of Pediatrics* 143, 386–93.

Wilson, J. (2005) 'Engaging Children and Young People: a Theatre of Possibilities', in Vetere, A. and Dowling, E. (eds) *Narrative Therapies with Children and their Families*. London: Routledge.

Winnicott, D. W. (1971) *Playing and Reality*. London: Routledge.

Winston's Wish (2000) *Muddles, Puddles and Sunshine*. Stroud: Hawthorn Press.

Winther Jørgensen, M. and Phillips, L. (2002) *Discourse Analysis as Theory and Method*. London: Sage.

Winthrop, A. L.; Brasel, S. L. and Woodgate, R. L. (2005) 'Siblings' Experiences with Childhood Cancer: a Different Way of Being in the Family', *Cancer Nursing* 29(5), 406–14.

Wolpin, B.; Chabner, B.; Lynch, T. and Penson, R. (2005) 'Learning to Cope: How Far is Too Close?' *Oncologist* 10(6), 449–56.

World Health Organization (2010) 'Definition of Palliative Care', www.who.int/cancer/pallaitive/definition/en/

Wouters, E.; van Loon, F.; van Rensburg, D. and Meulemans, H. (2009) 'Community Support and Disclosure of HIV Serostatus to Families by Public Sector Anti-Retroviral Patients in the Free State Province of South Africa', *AIDs Patient Care and STD* 23(5), 595–603.

Yancik, R. and Reis, L. A. G. (2000) 'Aging and Cancer in America: Demographic and Epidemiologic Perspectives', *Hematology/Oncology Clinics of America* 14(1), 17–23.

Yngvesson, B. and Mahoney, M. A. (2000) 'As One Should, Ought and Wants to Be', *Theory, Culture and Society* 17(6), 77–110.

Zebrack, B. J. (2000) 'Cancer Survivor Identity and Quality of Life', *Cancer Practice* 8(5), 238–42.

Index